Holiday Favorites

Presented by
California Home Economics Teachers

Editor
Donna Lyn Hulen

Photography Procured By
Gerry Murray Henderson

Graphics By
Laura Pierce

©Library of Congress Catalog
Card No. 83-072739
ISBN 0-914-159-01-1

©California Cookbook Company MCMLXXXV
116 So. Waterwheel Way, Orange, California 92669

HOLIDAY FAVORITES

Everybody loves Holidays! Usually it means good food, good fun, and being with good folks! Being the melting pot that it is, America celebrates about 32 different holidays (more or less, depending on who's counting!) throughout the calendar year.

In this collection of recipes from California Home Economics Teachers, you will find holiday recipes commemorating most of the holidays that occur throughout the year. Who are these "Professional Home Economists" who wrote these recipes? They are California Home Economics Teachers (with several recipe contributions coming from outside of California!) who understand teaching the culinary arts to others, in particular teaching those skills to students. Therefore, you will find these holiday recipes and instructions simple, direct, and applicable to use throughout the calendar year!

To all these recipe contributors whose names and schools appear beneath their recipes, we owe everything for the main content of this book. To Doug Pierce and Doug Herrema (my fine "cookbook cohorts") who spent many hours collecting these recipes . . . thanks, guys, you're sure fun to work with, and I sure think a lot of both of you!

To Laura Pierce, the graphics designer, we are grateful for many hours of creative artwork. To Donna Lyn Hulen, of Los Alamitos High School, we are thankful for many hours of laborious, careful editing on the recipes. To Gerry Murray Henderson, of Temple City High School, who procured and selected all the color photography used both on the front cover and throughout this book, we are most grateful for terrific quality color pictures.

Further, we express our gratitude to Baskin-Robbins, Kingsford's, Karo Corn Syrup, Best Foods, Hellman's, and, in particular, to Hershey's for all the color photography which you'll find within *Holiday Favorites*. We hope that you as the purchaser are pleased with the book, and we look forward to publishing others in the years to come.

GRADY W. REED   DOUG HERREMA   DOUG PIERCE

CALIFORNIA HOME ECONOMICS TEACHERS ADVISORY COMMITTEE

Anderson, Jill
Santa Paula High School, Santa Paula

Black-Eacker, Ellen
Nogales High School, La Puente

Cain, Joy Nell
Willowood Jr. H.S., West Covina

Estes, Marianne
La Mirada High School, La Mirada

Frank, Polly
Lakewood High School, Lakewood

Friederichsen, Jan
Vista Del Rio, Jr. H.S., Orange

Glennan, Renee
Sequoia Junior High School, Simi Valley

Henderson, Gerry
Temple City High School, Temple City

Hibma, Grace
Office of Los Angeles County Superintendent of Schools, Consultant, Consumer & Homemaking Education

Himenes, Peggy
Actis Junior High School, Bakersfield

Hulen Cheryl
Hemet High School, Hemet

Hulen, Donna Lyn
Los Alamitos High School, Los Alamitos

Huntzinger, Susan
Glendale High School, Glendale

Lash, Mary
Paramount High School, Paramount

Lundy, Jeri
Grossmont High School, Grossmont

Lopez, Karen
San Luis Obispo High School
San Luis Obispo

Marcus, Meridith
San Pasqual High School, Escondido

Matsuno, Dale
Montebello Intermediate School
Montebello

Mitchell, Eudora
Norwalk High School, Norwalk

Nelson, Peggy
Norte Vista High School, Riverside

Pace, Sally
Woodlake High School, Woodlake

Pendleton, Susie
Cerritos High School, Cerritos

Phipps, Louise
Washington Middle School, Vistra

Pereira, Marilyn
Hanford High School, Hanford

Priestley, Roberta
Alhambra High School, Alhambra

Pringle, Adrienne
Valley View Junior High School
Simi Valley

Rayl, Charla
El Toro High School, El Toro

Reza, Maria
Supervisor, Home Economics
Los Angeles Unified School District

Richmond, Mary E.
San Luis Obispo High School
San Luis Obispo

Ruth, Lynda
La Mirada High School, La Mirada

Shrock, Bonnie
Kearny High School, San Diego

Traw, Marianne
Ball Junior High School, Anaheim

West, Ruby
Elliott Junior High School, Pasadena

Wildermuth, Ellie
La Canada High School, La Canada

Wong, Pat
Taft High School, Taft

COLOR PHOTOGRAPHY CREDITS

Cover Photograph
Courtesy of Hershey's Foods Corporation, Hershey, PA.

Interior Photographs
Courtesy of Hershey's Food Corporation, Baskin Robbins, Kingsford's, Karo Corn Syrup, Best Foods, and Hellman's.

COLOR PHOTOGRAPHED RECIPES

TO ORDER ADDITIONAL COPIES OF "HOLIDAY FAVORITES"

Send name, address and $7.80 (includes tax and postage) to:

California Cookbook Company, 116 So. Waterwheel Way, Orange, CA 92669

Other books available at $7.80 (includes tax and postage) are:

Sweet Surprises
International Cuisine
A Matter of Taste

Those available at $6.75 (includes tax and postage) are:

Fiesta Favorites
Light Cuisine
Simple Selections

─Contents─

(Includes: Lincoln's Birthday, Washington's Birthday, Memorial Day, Fourth of July, Labor Day)

On our cover:

A. Chocoberry Torte, page 112.

B. Double Chocolate Delight, page 112.

Courtesy of Hershey's

Halloween

Cheese Witches

Serves 12

1½ cups American cheese, grated
¼ cup tomato sauce
1 teaspoon Worcestershire sauce
2 drops Tabasco sauce

1 teaspoon chili powder
6 English muffins, split in half
½ cup crushed Fritos

In a small mixing bowl, mix cheese, tomato sauce, Worcestershire sauce, Tobasco and chili powder. Spread mixture on the split English muffins and sprinkle crushed Fritos on top. Place on rack, so that buns are 3″ below broiler unit. Broil until cheese is melted. (Careful not to burn Fritos.)

"This is a favorite among our teenagers in our foods lab. We serve a Halloween buffet with cider punch, a cheese ball and vegetables."

Sandra Robertson   **Whittier High School**
                                                          Whittier

Best-Ever Cornbread

Serves 6

2 cups Bisquick
¾ cup sugar
¼ cup yellow cornmeal
1 teaspoon baking powder

2 eggs, slightly beaten
¾ cube soft margarine
1 cup evaporated milk

Preheat oven to 350⁰.

Mix Bisquick, sugar, cornmeal and baking powder with a fork. Slightly beat eggs, margarine, and evaporated milk. Add to the Bisquick mixture and stir only until dry ingredients are moistened. Pour into a 9″ x 13″ baking pan and bake for 30 to 35 minutes. Cut and serve hot.

Alice Mittermiller   **La Jolla High School**
                                                          La Jolla

Southwestern Corn Chowder

Serves 2

3 slices of bacon
¼ cup onion, chopped
½ potato, diced
¼ cup water
½ can cream style corn
½ can cream of mushroom soup

½ small can mushrooms
1 cup milk
½ teaspoon salt
1 cup green chili, chopped
    (fresh, if possible)

Cook bacon in a large skillet or sauce pan. Remove and drain. Pour off drippings returning 3 tablespoons to pan. Add onion and potato and cook until onion is lightly browned. Add water, cover and simmer until potatoes are tender. Stir in corn, soup, mushrooms, milk and salt; heat to a boil; lower heat. Add chili and simmer a minute or two. Crumble bacon over chowder and serve with grilled cheese sandwich.

Olivia Romero   **Valley High School**
Albuquerque, New Mexico

Halloween Jello Salad

Serves 8

1 6-oz. package orange gelatin
2 cups boiling water
1 pint orange sherbet

1 small can mandarin oranges, drained
1 can crushed pineapple, drained
2 bananas, sliced

Dissolve gelatin in boiling water; add sherbet. Whip with rotary beater until light and fluffy. Add mandarin oranges, pineapple and bananas. Mix. Chill until firm.

"This can be used for any fall occasion."

Cheryl Sakahara

Piute School
Lancaster

Jolly Jacko Cups

Serves 10

1½ pounds ground beef
1 onion, chopped
1 tablespoon chili powder
1 teaspoon cumin
½ teaspoon salt
¼ teaspoon garlic salt

1 15-oz. can tomato sauce
1 cup carrots, grated
1 4-oz. can olives, chopped
1 10-oz. can refrigerator biscuits
10 slices processed cheese

Brown beef and onion in a large skillet. Drain fat. Add chili powder, cumin and garlic. Stir in tomato sauce, carrot and olives. Cover and cook over low heat 20 minutes, stirring occasionally.

Roll each biscuit on a lightly floured surface, making a 4" circle. Grease the bottom of a muffin pan and press biscuit to the bottom of the pan, making a cup. Bake at 400° for 10 minutes or until lightly browned. Remove cups from pan immediately.

Place cups on a cookie sheet. Fill each cup with meat mixture. Cut cheese slices into 3" circles. From these circles, cut a Jack-o-lantern face, triangle eyes, nose and smiling mouth. Place "face" over meat filled cup. Return to oven until cheese begins to melt, about 2 minutes.

"Fun, nutritious dinner for trick or treaters!"

Nanci Burkhart

Hueneme High School
Oxnard

Dinner-in-a-Pumpkin

Serves 6

1 8 to 10 pound pumpkin
1½ pounds ground beef
1 small onion, chopped
1 clove garlic, minced
1½ teaspoons sugar
1½ teaspoons mixed Italian herbs

1½ teaspoons salt
⅛ teaspoon pepper
4 cups tomato juice
3 cups shredded cabbage
½ pound green beans, cut up
1 cup uncooked rice

Wash pumpkin, cut off top, scrape out seeds and discard. Cook ground beef slightly, drain off fat, add onion, garlic and saute slightly. Add seasonings and tomato juice and heat. Mix with uncooked rice.

3

Shred cabbage and cut green beans. Layer 1/3 each of the cabbage, green beans, rice and meat mixture in the pumpkin. Repeat layers and replace lid. Bake at 350⁰ for 2½ to 3 hours or until done. (Pumpkin is done when it is soft when pierced with a fork.)

Slice and serve with tossed green salad and corn bread.

"This is a perfect Halloween 'make ahead' dinner for that busy 'Trick or treat' evening.

Alice Mittermiller   ***La Jolla High School***
La Jolla

Halloween Chili Bake

Serves 4 to 5

1 pound hamburger	*8 oz. longhorn cheddar cheese, grated*
1 15-oz. can chili con carne with beans	*1 small bag Fritos*
1 15-oz. can chili con carne without beans	

Cook hamburger in skillet until brown, drain. Add the chili and heat. Alternate in a casserole dish, a layer of meat mixture, layer of grated cheese, and a layer of fritos. Repeat process until casserole is filled, putting extra Fritos and cheese on top. Place in a 350⁰ oven until cheese melts and fritos are crisp.

"This dish is quick and easy to prepare for a ski trip!"

Joyce Grohmann   ***Bellflower High School***
Bellflower

Caramel Popcorn

Makes 4 quarts

1 cup sugar	*½ teaspoon vanilla*
½ cup margarine	*4 quarts popped corn*
1 cup dark corn syrup	*1 cup peanuts*
½ teaspoon salt	

Combine sugar, margarine, syrup, salt and vanilla in a 1½ quart sauce pan. Stir and boil for 5 minutes.

Put popped corn in a shallow baking pan. Pour above mixture over popcorn. Add peanuts and stir well. Bake in a 250⁰ oven, stirring every 15 minutes for about an hour. Cool and break apart.

Millie Walls   ***El Dorado High School***
Placentia

Taffy Apples

Serves 6

6 medium apples	*2 tablespoons butter*
1 cup sugar	*dash of salt*
1 cup light corn syrup	*½ teaspoon vanilla*
1 cup half and half	*walnuts, finely chopped (optional)*

4

Wash and dry apples. Insert skewers in stem of each apple. Combine sugar, corn syrup and half and half in large saucepan. Cook rapidly, stirring constantly to 245° on candy thermometer. Remove from heat at once.

Stir in butter, salt and vanilla. Dip apples quickly, first in syrup, then in chopped nuts, if desired. Place on buttered sheet to cool. Cool thoroughly.

Nancy Jordan   **Merced High School**
Merced

Pumpkin-Eater Doughnuts

Makes 2 dozen

2 tablespoons shortening	2¾ cups flour
¾ cup sugar	2 teaspoons baking powder
2 eggs	1 teaspoon pumpkin pie spice
1 cup canned pumpkin	½ teaspoon salt
1 cup shredded bran cereal	vegetable oil
	cinnamon/sugar

Beat shortening and sugar together until fluffy. Beat in eggs, one at a time. Stir in pumpkin and then cereal. Let stand 2 minutes. Sift flour, baking powder, spice and salt together. Stir into pumpkin mixture. Cover and chill one hour or until stiff enough to handle.

Roll to ½" thick on a lightly floured board. Cut. Fry until golden brown. Dip into cinnamon/sugar.

Loretta Salau   **Foothill High School**
Bakersfield

Orange Glazed Pumpkin Muffins

Makes 12

1-2/3 cups flour	1 egg, beaten
½ cup sugar	¼ cup salad oil
1 tablespoon baking powder	½ cup canned pumpkin
½ teaspoon salt	2/3 cup undiluted evaporated milk
½ teaspoon cinnamon	¼ cup orange marmalade or substitute
½ teaspoon nutmeg	glaze

Sift flour, sugar, baking powder, salt, cinnamon and nutmeg into medium bowl. Mix thoroughly. In a separate bowl, mix together egg, oil and pumpkin. Add the milk and mix well. Mix the flour mixture and the pumpkin mixture together until dry ingredients are moistened. Spoon into 12 buttered muffin cups and place 1 level teaspoon marmalade on top of each muffin. Bake at 400° for 20 to 25 minutes. Remove from pan immediately. Place on wire rack to cool.

Lou Helen Yergat   **Mission Viejo High School**
Mission Viejo

Pumpkin Spice Cupcakes

Serves 12

¼ cup shortening
½ cup plus 2 tablespoons sugar
1 egg
1 cup plus 2 tablespoons flour
1¼ teaspoon baking powder
¼ teaspoon baking soda
½ teaspoon salt

1 teaspoon cinnamon
¼ teaspoon ginger
¼ teaspoon nutmeg
½ cup pumpkin
1/3 cup milk
cupcake papers

Cream shortening and sugar until light and fluffy. Beat eggs separately and blend into sugar and shortening. Measure flour, baking powder, baking soda, salt, cinnamon, ginger and nutmeg into separate bowl. Sift. Sift again.

Mix pumpkin and milk in a separate bowl. Add dry ingredients alternately with pumpkin mixture to sugar, shortening and egg.

Pour batter into lined muffin tins, filling each ¾ full. Bake at 350⁰ for 25 to 30 minutes.

Orange Frosting
¼ cup margarine
1½ cup powdered sugar
1 egg yolk

¼ teaspoon vanilla
1 tablespoon orange juice concentrate

Cream margarine with wooden spoon. Sift powdered sugar and gradually add to margarine.

Separate egg yolk from white. Add yolk to margarine and powdered sugar. Stir in orange juice and vanilla. Frost cupcakes.

Terri Pratt

*Sage School
Palmdale*

Pumpkin Cake Roll

Serves 8

3 eggs
1 cup sugar
2/3 cup pumpkin
1 teaspoon lemon juice
¾ cup flour
1 teaspoon baking powder
2 teaspoons cinnamon
1 teaspoon ginger

½ teaspoon salt
½ teaspoon nutmeg
1 cup finely chopped walnuts
1 cup powdered sugar
2 3-oz. packages cream cheese
4 tablespoons butter
½ teaspoons vanilla

Beat eggs on high speed of mixer for 5 minutes, gradually beat in sugar. Stir in pumpkin and lemon juice. In a separate bowl, mix together flour, baking powder, salt and spices. Fold into pumpkin mixture. Spread into a greased and floured 1" x 10" x 15" jelly roll pan. Top with walnuts. Bake at 375⁰ for 15 minutes. Turn out on a towel sprinkled with powdered sugar. Starting at narrow end, roll towel and cake together. Cool. Unroll, then fill.

Filling
Combine 1 cup powdered sugar, softened cream cheese, butter and vanilla. Beat until smooth. Spread over cake. Re-roll. Chill. Serve.

Mary Cronkhite
6

*Antelope Valley
Lancaster*

Choco-Dot Pumpkin Cake

Serves 12 to 16

2 cups flour	2 cups sugar
2 teaspoons baking powder	4 eggs
1 teaspoon baking soda	1 1-pound can pumpkin
½ teaspoon salt	1 cup vegetable oil
1½ teaspoons cinnamon	1 cup All Bran cereal
½ teaspoon cloves	6 oz. chocolate chips
¼ teaspoon allspice	1 cup nuts, chopped
¼ teaspoon ginger	

Combine dry ingredients and set aside. In a large bowl, beat eggs until foamy. Add pumpkin, oil and All-Bran; mix well. Add dry ingredients, mixing just until combined. Stir in chocolate chips and nuts. Spread in ungreased Bundt pan. Bake at 350⁰ for 1 hour 10 minutes. Cool before removing from pan.

"This is so good, it doesn't even need frosting!"

Penny Niadna

Golden West High School
Visalia

Pumpkin-Shaped Cake

Serves 8 to 12

1 angel food cake mix	dash of salt
1½ cups granulated sugar	1 teaspoon vanilla
1/3 cup cold water	green and orange food coloring
2 egg whites	1 banana
2 teaspoons light corn syrup or ¼ teaspoon cream of tartar	

Mix cake according to directions on package. Pour batter into a large oiled and floured Pyrex mixing bowl. Bake according to instructions on package. Invert bowl to cool and remove cake.

Frosting
Mix sugar, water, egg whites, corn syrup or cream of tartar, and salt in top of double boiler. Beat ½ minute on low speed of electric mixer. Place over boiling water and cook about seven minutes while beating constantly on high speed of electric mixer or until stiff peaks form.

Remove from heat; add vanilla and beat until of spreading consistency (2 to 3 minutes). Remove ½ cup of the frosting. Add a few drops of orange food coloring to remaining frosting.

Cut a little of the cake away to get pumpkin shape. Frost with orange frosting, bringing spatula from bottom to top to make it look like ridges in a pumpkin.

Cut 3" from end of banana and secure it into frosting to look like stem. Add green food coloring to the ½ cup remaining frosting and frost the stem.

"Beautiful!"

Alice Mittermiller

La Jolla High School
La Jolla

Bewitching Raisin Dunkers

Serves 10 to 12

3 cups biscuit mix
1 egg
½ to ¾ cup water
½ teaspoon cinnamon
½ cup raisins, chopped

½ cup sugar
¼ teaspoon cinnamon
¼ teaspoon nutmeg

Beat egg. Add biscuit mix, cinnamon, nutmeg, raisins and water. Stir to make soft dough using a wooden spoon. Turn onto lightly floured board. Knead lightly just until smooth. Roll out into a rectangle (8″ x 10″). Using doughnut cutter, cut 8 to 10 doughnut shapes. Reroll dough to cut extra shapes or shape dough as desired. Bake on greased cookie sheet 20 minutes. Brush with melted butter; sprinkle with cinnamon and sugar.

Alternative Cooking Method
Fry in deep preheated oil (375⁰) until golden on both sides. Drain on paper toweling. While still warm, roll in cinnamon and sugar.

Sydney Fox   *Orange Glen High School*
                                                                Escondido

Kookie Cookie Owls

Makes 2 dozen

2/3 cup margarine
1 cup brown sugar
1 egg
1 teaspoon vanilla
1 cup crunchy peanut butter
1-1/3 cups flour
1 teaspoon baking pwoder

½ teaspoon salt
1 cup uncooked oatmeal
1 oz. unsweetened chocolate, melted
chocolate chips
whole cashew nuts

Beat margarine and sugar together until creamy. Add egg, vanilla and peanut butter. Blend thoroughly. Sift together flour, baking powder and salt. Add to mixture. Blend well. Stir in oatmeal. Divide dough in half. Shape one half to form a roll 8″ long. Add chocolate to other half. Roll out chocolate dough on waxed paper to form an 8″ square. Place roll on chocolate dough. Wrap chocolate dough around roll. Pinch seam together. Wrap in waxed paper. Chill at least one hour.

Cut ¼″ slices. For each owl face, pinch chocolate dough to form "ears." Use 2 chocolate chips for eyes and cashew for beak. Place on an ungreased cookie sheet. Bake at 350⁰ for 12 to 15 minutes.

Phyllis Kaylor   *Ray Kroc Middle School*
                                                                 San Diego

Molasses Witch Cookies

Serves Several Trick or Treaters

½ cup shortening
½ cup sugar
½ cup unsulphured molasses
1 egg yolk
2 cups sifted all-purpose flour
½ teaspoon salt

½ teaspoon baking soda
1 teaspoon baking powder
1 teaspoon cloves
1 teaspoon ginger
1½ teaspoon cinnamon
½ teaspoon nutmeg

8

Cream together shortening, sugar and molasses. Add egg yolk; mix well. Sift together flour, salt, baking soda, baking powder and spices. Stir into molasses mixture. Mix well and chill.

Roll out ¼" thick and cut out 2½" round shapes, then cut into triangles. Press triangle into edge of round for hats. Cut out strips of licorice for base of hat and facial features. Bake at 350⁰ for 8 to 10 minutes.

Cleone Hatwan   *Paramount High School*
                                                              Paramount

Pumpkin Face Cookie
Makes 18

Dough
¾ cup shortening
½ cup brown sugar, packed
1 egg
¼ cup light molasses
2 cups all-purpose flour
½ teaspoon baking soda
½ cup oatmeal, ground up in blender
1 teaspoon salt

Filling
½ cup canned pumpkin
½ cup sugar
½ teaspoon ground cinnamon
½ teaspoon ground ginger
¼ teaspoon ground nutmeg

Dough
Cream shortening and brown sugar; beat in egg and molasses. Mix flour, baking soda, oatmeal and 1 teaspoon salt. Stir into creamed mixture. Put dough in small bowl and chill.

Filling
Mix together, canned pumpkin, sugar, cinnamon, ginger and nutmeg. Cook and stir until bubbly. Cool.

On floured surface, roll dough ⅛" thick. Cut into 36 3" circles. (Use biscuit cutters.) Place a teaspoon of pumpkin filling atop half the circles. Place on ungreased cookie sheet. Cut faces in remaining circles. Place atop filling. Seal edges with fork. Press on stems cut from dough scrapes. Bake at 375⁰ for 12 minutes.

Note: Be sure you use all the filling and roll dough thin enough to make 36 circles, otherwise cookies are too dry. The cookie is 2 layers thick. The filling is in between the 2 cookie layers. Roll out the dough and cut the circles as close together as possible, so you won't have to keep re-rolling the dough.

Gloria King   *Schurr High School*
                                                            Montebello

Pumpkin Spice Cookies
Makes 9 dozen

2¼ cups sugar
¾ cup shortening
2 eggs, well beaten
1 large can pumpkin
1¼ teaspoons baking soda
4 cups sifted flour
4 teaspoons baking powder
2 cups raisins

1 cup nuts, chopped
½ teaspoon ginger
½ teaspoon cinnamon
½ teaspoon allspice
¼ teaspoon cloves
1 teaspoon salt
2 teaspoons vanilla

Cream together sugar and shortening. Add eggs, pumpkin and baking soda. Mix in all remaining ingredients and stir well. Drop from teaspoon onto cookie sheet. Sprinkle with cinnamon sugar. Bake at 375⁰ for 8 to 10 minutes.

"Our FHA made these cookies for a children's party. Omit the raisins and nuts and make large cookies using a ¼ cup measuring cup. Top with cream cheese frosting and decorate with candy corn and raisins to make pumpkin faces."

Sue Roa Hope   *Lompoc Valley Middle School*
                                                                    Lompoc

Peanut Butter Piece Cookies

Makes about 4 dozen

2/3 cup butter or margarine	½ cup unsweetened cocoa
1 cup sugar	½ teaspoon baking powder
1 egg	¼ teaspoon salt
1½ teaspoons vanilla	1/3 cup milk
1-2/3 cups unsifted all-purpose flour	1 cup candy coated peanut butter pieces (Reese's pieces)

Cream butter, sugar, egg and vanilla until light and fluffy. Combine flour, cocoa, baking powder and salt; add alternately with milk to creamed mixture. Stir in ½ cup peanut butter pieces. Drop by teaspoonsful 2" apart onto lightly greased cookie sheet. Bake at 350⁰ for 7 to 9 minutes or until set, but not dry. Cool slightly; remove from cookie sheet onto wire rack. (Photo page 10)

Hershey Foods Corporation   *Hershey, PA*

Peanut Butter Piece Oatmeal Bars

Makes about 20 bars

2/3 cup shortening	½ teaspoon baking soda
½ cup packed brown sugar	½ teaspoon salt
1/3 cup sugar	¼ cup milk
1 egg	1½ cups rolled oats
½ teaspoon vanilla	1¼ cups candy coated peanut butter pieces (Reese's pieces)
1 cup unsifted all-purpose flour	

Cream shortening, brown sugar and sugar until light and fluffy; beat in egg and vanilla. Combine flour, baking soda and salt; add alternately with milk to cream mixture. Stir in rolled oats and ½ cup peanut butter pieces. Spoon into greased 13" x 9" x 2" pan spreading evenly; sprinkle with remaining peanut butter pieces. Bake at 350⁰ for 30 to 35 minutes or until almost no imprint remains when lightly touched in center. Cool; cut into bars. (Photo page 10)

Peanut Butter Cookies
Drop batter by teaspoonsful onto a lightly greased cookie sheet. Place 3 or 4 peanut butter pieces near center of each cookie. Bake to375⁰ for 10 to 12 minutes or until light brown.

Makes about 3 dozen cookies.

Hershey Foods Corporation   *Hershey, PA*

Recipe for "Peanut Butter Piece Cookies" on page 10 ➜
Recipe for "Peanut Butter Piece Oatmeal Bars" on page 10 ➜

Thanksgiving

…pe for "Light Herb Turkey Gravy" on page 19

Crab and Cheese Fondue

Serves 6 to 8 (as an appetizer)

2 tablespoons butter
2 tablespoons flour
1 cup canned chicken broth
¼ cup sherry
dash onion salt

3 to 4 drops hot pepper sauce
1 8-oz. package cream cheese
¼ pound processed American cheese
1 6-oz. can or frozen crab meat

Melt butter in a fondue pot over medium heat. Stir in flour. Add chicken broth, sherry, salt and pepper sauce. Cook and stir until thick. Add cheeses, stirring until all cheese has melted. Add crab meat and stir. Reduce heat to low to serve. Use French bread cubes for dippers.

Kitty Worley   *Norte Vista High School*
Riverside

Stuffed Mushroom Appetizers

Makes 36 medium sized appetizers

1 pound mushrooms
1 10-oz. package frozen chopped spinach
1 cup cottage cheese
1 clove garlic, minced

1/3 cup grated parmesian cheese
melted butter, optional
pepper to taste

Remove stems from mushrooms, mince. Brush caps with melted butter, if desired. Combine spinach, cottage cheese, garlic, stems and pepper. Spoon into caps. Top with parmesian cheese. Bake at 400⁰ for 10 minutes.

Kathryn Phillips   *Lincoln Middle School*
Vista

Thanksgiving Pate

Serves 4

1 cooked turkey liver, minced
2 hard cooked eggs, minced

1 teaspoon Lawry's Seasoned Salt
1 to 2 tablespoons mayonnaise

Combine first three ingredients and add mayonnaise gradually, until mixture is spreadable. Serve surrounded by tiny slices of party rye bread.

Carol Lovett   *Horace Ensign School*
Newport Beach

Never-Fail Cranberry Jelly

Serves 8 to 10

4 cups fresh cranberries
2 cups boiling water

2 cups sugar
dash of salt

Pick over and wash cranberries. Combine cranberries, water and salt in a two quart saucepan. Bring to a boil and simmer 20 minutes. Remove and rub through a sieve. Return to stove and cook 3 minutes (at a full rolling boil) Add sugar and cook 2 minutes. Mold and chill.

"For Christmas, use a star shaped mold or individual star molds."

Marguerite S. Darnall   *Corona Senior High School*
Corona

Cranberry Candles

Serves 12

2 1-pound cans whole cranberry sauce
1½ cups boiling water
1 package cherry gelatin
¼ teaspoon salt
1 tablespoon lemon juice

½ cup mayonnaise
1 orange, peeled and sliced
¼ cup nuts, chopped
12 6-oz. empty fruit juice cans

Heat cranberry sauce in a saucepan, strain, and set aside.

Combine hot juice and water, and add gelatin stirring until dissolved. Add salt and lemon juice. Chill. When slightly thickened, beat in mayonnaise until light and fluffy. Fold in cranberries, fruits and nuts. Divide mixture evenly into juice cans. Chill 4 hours or more. Unmold on festive greens. Insert small wax birthday candles into the tops and flame.

Carol Lovett

Horace Ensign School
Newport Beach

Cranberry-Orange Nut Mold

Serves 6

2 cups fresh cranberries
1 orange, peeled and quartered
½ cup seedless raisins
¾ cup walnuts, chopped

1 package strawberry gelatin
¾ to 1 cup sugar
1 cup boiling water
5 ice cubes

Put cranberries, orange and raisins through food chopper or whirl in food processor until coarsely ground. Turn out into bowl. Add chopped walnuts and mix well.

In a medium sized bowl, dissolve 1 package strawberry gelatin in 1 cup boiling water. Stir in sugar. Add 5 ice cubes and stir until dissolved. Stir in chopped ingredients and place in mold. Refrigerate. When firm, unmold on a bed of lettuce.

"Great with turkey and dressing!"

Vera Wilson

Del Dios Middle School
Escondido

Cranberry Raspberry Salad

Serves 8 to 9

1 3-oz. package raspberry gelatin
¾ cup boiling water
1 10-oz. package frozen raspberries
½ teaspoon lemon juice
½ pint sour cream

1 3-oz. package cherry gelatin
½ cup boiling water
1 8½-oz. can crushed pineapple
1 can (½ pound) whole berry cranberry sauce

Dissolve raspberry gelatin in boiling water, and add frozen raspberries and lemon juice. Stir to thaw raspberries which chills the gelatin. Pour into a 9″ x 9″ pan and refrigerate until firm, then cover with half pint of sour cream.

Meanwhile, dissolve cherry gelatin in boiling water and add pineapple and cranberry sauce, mixing thoroughly. Allow mixture to chill and thicken slightly. Then pour on top of sour cream and chill thoroughly before serving.

Jan Neufeld

Fullerton High School

Cranberry Waldorf Salad

Serves 8 to 10

½ pound cranberries, ground
¾ cup sugar
2 cups mini marshmallows
2 cups apples, diced

½ cup grapes, quartered
½ cup nuts, chopped
½ teaspoon salt
1 cup whipping cream, whipped

Grind cranberries, add sugar and marshmallows. Let stand overnight in the refrigerator. Add remaining ingredients, stirring into cranberry mixture. Refrigerate, then serve.

Rita Matthews   **Hillcrest School**
                                                     Redondo Beach

Cranberry Fruit Salad

Serves 12

4 cups fresh cranberries
2 cups sugar
1 cup red grapes, halved

1 cup crushed pineapple
½ cup nuts
½ pint whipped cream

Grind cranberries and mix well with sugar. Let stand for 1 hour, then add red grapes without seeds and crushed pineapple. Chill overnight. Add ½ cup nuts and re-chill.

Just before serving, fold in whipped cream.

Wilma Reaser   **Hemet Junior High School**
                                            Hemet

Sweet Potatoes Alexander

Serves 6

¾ cups butter
½ cup sugar
½ cup orange juice
1/3 cup orange liqueur
1 large apple, sliced

2 cups sweet potatoes, cooked and sliced
1 cup peaches, sliced
2 bananas, sliced
¼ cup almonds, sliced

In a small saucepan, melt butter and sugar over low heat. When melted, add orange juice and liqueur. Remove from heat.

Place sauce in the bottom of a baking dish and add layers of apples, sweet potatoes, peaches and bananas. Sprinkle almonds on top. Bake at 350⁰ for 25 minutes.

"A dish liked even by those who don't like sweet potatoes!"

Susie Pendleton   **Cerritos High School**
                                                 Cerritos

Sweet Potato Casserole

Serves 8 to 10

1 40-oz. can sweet potatoes, mashed
½ cup margarine
1 cup granulated sugar
2 eggs, beaten
1/3 cup evaporated milk
1 teaspoon vanilla

Topping
1 cup brown sugar
1/3 cup margarine
1/3 cup flour
1 cup pecans, chopped

Drain juice off sweet potatoes and mash. Add margarine, granulated sugar, eggs, evaporated milk, and vanilla to the sweet potatoes. Place in a greased pan or casserole dish.

Mix topping ingredients together and spread on top of the sweet potatoes. Bake at 350⁰ for 25 to 30 minutes.

"Rich and easy to make. A family favorite."

Susan Lefler   *Ramona Junior High School*
Chino

Pecan Sweet Potatoes

Serves 8 to 10

2½ to 3 pounds sweet potatoes or yams,
    cooked and peeled
2 eggs
¾ cup brown sugar
½ cup melted butter

1 teaspoon salt
1 teaspoon cinnamon
1 cup orange juice
1 cup pecan halves

Mash sweet potatoes. Beat in eggs, ¼ cup brown sugar, ¼ cup of the melted butter, salt and cinnamon. If potatoes seem dry, beat in orange juice until moist and fluffy. Put in a 1½ or 2 quart casserole dish.

Before baking, arrange pecan halves on top and sprinkle with remaining ½ cup brown sugar. Then drizzle with remaining ¼ cup melted butter. Bake uncovered at 375⁰ for 20 minutes or until heated through.

Willy Hall   *McPherson Junior High School*
Orange

Make-Ahead Mashed Potatoes

Serves 8

6 cups mashed potatoes
3 cups cream style cottage cheese
¾ cup sour cream
1½ tablespoons onion, finely chopped

2½ teaspoons salt
⅛ teaspoon white pepper
butter
slivered almonds

Use very little butter and no milk when mashing the potatoes. Stir in the remaining ingredients. Dot with butter and slivered almonds and bake at 350⁰ for 30 minutes.

Brenda Umbro   *San Marcos Junior High School*
San Marcos

Bird-in-a-Bag

Serves - Depends on size of turkey

½ cup shortening
1 heavy brown paper bag
staples

roasting pan with rack
1 turkey, scrubbed, stuffed and tied

Starting at the bottom of the bag, rub shortening all over the bottom and up the sides. (May need more shortening.) Cover generously.

Butter outside of turkey after it has been scrubbed, stuffed and tied. Place turkey in bag. Breast side of turkey should be up and seam in bag should be on top. Fold over ends of bag as many times as possible. Staple the bag shut. Place turkey on rack in roasting pan. Roast undisturbed according to following time table.

8 - 12 lbs. 2½ - 3 hours
12 - 16 lbs. 3 - 3¾ hours
16 - 20 lbs. 3¾ - 4½ hours
20 - 24 lbs. 4½ - 5½ hours

When done, puncture bag around bottom carefully allowing steam to escape. Cut away rest of bag and poke holes in bottom of bag to allow juices to fall into roasting pan. Transfer turkey to heated platter and keep warm in oven while you make the gravy in roasting pan.

"So easy, so moist, you won't believe it! New England Bread stuffing is perfect in this turkey!"

Mary E. Richmond   **San Luis Obispo High School**
                                                       San Luis Obispo

New England Bread Stuffing

Makes enough stuffing for one 14 - 16 lb. bird

2 12-oz. bags prepared bread dressing mix
1½ cups diced celery and leaves
2 medium onions, cut up very fine
2 tablespoons parsley flakes
1 teaspoon oregano

½ teaspoon thyme
1 teaspoon sage
2 tablespoons poultry seasoning
1 cup melted butter or margarine
1 cup broth or water

Mix first eight ingredients together. Stir in melted butter and half of the broth or water. Blend lightly until moistened. Test moistness by squeezing small amount of stuffing in hand and if it retains its shape, it is moist enough. If it crumbles add rest of broth until it holds together.

Stuff neck cavity first and secure with small skewer or "turkey pins." Pack rest of stuffing into body cavity and seal with the heel of a loaf of bread. Tie legs and wings together and prepare turkey for roasting.

Mary E. Richmond   **San Luis Obispo High School**
                                                       San Luis Obispo

Herbed Stuffing Balls

Serves 12

3 cups chicken broth
¾ pound butter or margarine (3 sticks)
1 medium onion, minced
½ cup parsley, minced
2 14-oz. bags Pepperridge Farm
  Herb Stuffing Mix

1 tablespoon fresh sage or 1½ teaspoon
  dried sage
½ teaspoon salt
½ teaspoon pepper
1½ teaspoon poultry seasoning
6 egg whites

In a large skillet or dutch oven, heat the chicken broth with the butter until butter has melted. Add remaining ingredients, except egg whites, and toss until evenly mixed. Beat the egg whites in a small bowl until frothy and pour over stuffing mixture. Toss to combine.

Using your hands, form the mixture into about 30 balls, measuring about 2½" in diameter. Place slightly apart on an oiled cookie sheet. Bake uncovered at 350° for 25 minutes.

To Prepare in Advance
Prepare up to 2 days before the party. It is best to wrap them in sets of 4 in plastic wrap to prevent drying. Bake just before serving. Leftover servings may be reheated, wrapped in foil to prevent drying.

Shirley A. Wilcox   **Burbank High School**
                                         Burbank

Apple-Stuffed Chicken Breasts

Serves 6

6 whole chicken breasts, skinned,
  boned and split
2 medium apples, peeled and cored
6 tablespoons butter or margarine
1 medium onion, finely chopped
1 clove garlic, minced
1 cup soft bread crumbs

1 teaspoon salt
½ teaspoon rosemary
½ teaspoon basil
flour
¾ cup apple juice
2 tablespoons cognac or sherry
cornstarch, optional

Place chicken between sheets or plastic wrap and pound with mallet until thin. Grate apples and set aside. Melt 3 tablespoons butter in large skillet. Saute onion and garlic until tender. Stir in apple, bread crumbs, salt, rosemary and basil. Stir over low heat until thoroughly mixed.

Spoon 2 or 3 tablespoons apple mixture onto boned side of each chicken breast. Roll up, tucking in ends and secure with wooden toothpick. Coat each with flour. Heat 3 tablespoons butter in clean skillet to assure better browning. Add apple juice and cognac or sherry. Simmer covered for 25 to 30 minutes. Place chicken on warm platter. Thicken pan juices with cornstarch dissolved in water to make a sauce. Pour sauce over chicken and garnish with parsley.

Donna Lyn Hulen   **Los Alamitos High School**
                                      Los Alamitos

Chicken California

Serves 6

4 tablespoons butter or margarine
4 tablespoons flour
½ teaspoon salt
¼ teaspoon pepper
2 cups milk

2 cups chicken, cooked, and cut in
   bite size pieces
2 cups Jack cheese, grated
1 dozen flour tortillas (medium)
2 tablespoons parsley, chopped

Melt butter in a saucepan over low heat. Blend in flour, salt and pepper all at once. Cook over low heat or lift up from heat, stirring until mixture is smooth and bubbly. Remove from heat. Stir in milk and heat to boiling, stirring constantly until smooth and thickened. (This makes 2 cups white sauce.)

Reserve one cup of cheese and sauce and set aside. Put a spoonful of chicken, cheese, and sauce in each tortilla and roll up enchilada style. Place in a 9″ x 13″ casserole dish. Spread evenly with remaining cup of sauce. Sprinkle with cheese and chopped parsley. Bake uncovered at 350° for 20 to 25 minutes.

Variation:
Add other ingredients to filling, such as chopped green chilies or use cooked turkey instead of chicken. Great as a Thanksgiving leftover!

Susan Dever   **Bishop Union High School**
Bishop

Oven-Fried Chicken Parmesian

Serves 3 to 4

½ cup parmesian cheese
¼ cup flour
1 teaspoon paprika
½ teaspoon salt
dash of pepper

2½ to 3 pound broiler-fryer, cut up
1 egg, slightly beaten
1 tablespoon milk
¼ cup margarine, melted

Combine cheese, flour and seasonings. Dip chicken in combined egg and milk. Coat with cheese mixture. Place in a baking dish and pour margarine over chicken. Bake at 350° for 1 hour or until tender.

Elizabeth A. Iorillo   **James Monroe Junior High School**
Ridgecrest

Turkey Gumbo

Serves 4

2 tablespoons cornstarch
1 cup water
1 tablespoon soy sauce
1 can condensed chicken gumbo soup
2 cups cubed cooked turkey

2 tablespoons pimento, chopped
½ cup celery, chopped
1 3-oz. can (2¼ cups) chow mein noodles
¼ cup water chestnuts, optional

In a sauce pan, combine cornstarch, water, soy sauce and soup. Cook, stirring constantly, until mixture is thickened and bubbly. Stir in the turkey, pimento, and celery and heat through. Serve over chow mein noodles.

"When you need a change from turkey sandwiches, try this!"

Carolyn Crum   **Newhart Junior High School**
Mission Viejo

Light Herb Turkey Gravy

Makes about 5 cups

Turkey giblets and neck
10 cups water
3 onions, peeled, quartered
3 ribs celery, cut into sticks
3 carrots, peeled, cut into sticks
1 to 2 teaspoons salt

3 chicken-flavored bouillon cubes
3 bay leaves
1/3 cup corn starch
1 teaspoon dried tarragon leaves
1 cup dry white wine

In a large saucepan place turkey giblets and neck, water, onion, celery, carrots, salt, bouillon cubes and bay leaves. Bring to a boil; reduce heat and simmer 1½ hours or until liquid is reduced by half. Drain broth; reserve.

Pour pan drippings into large measuring cup. Allow to stand several minutes until fat drippings separate from turkey juices. Discard fat drippings. Add reserved broth to turkey juices to equal 4 cups. Return to roasting pan. Stir together corn starch, tarragon and white wine until smooth; add to roasting pan. Stirring constantly, bring to a boil over medium heat, stirring up brown bits from bottom of pan and boil 1 minute.

Kingsford's, Best Foods,
Consumer Service Department

Englewood Cliffs,
New Jersey

Apple-Nut Bread

Serves a group — makes 1 loaf

1½ cups flour
2 teaspoons baking powder
½ teaspoon salt
½ teaspoon baking soda
½ teaspoon cinnamon
½ cup walnuts
1 cup crispy bran squares,
    (bite-sized)

1 egg
½ cup sour cream
¼ cup milk
¼ cup oil
1 teaspoon vanilla
1 cup apples, peeled and chopped
¾ cup brown sugar, packed
½ cup raisins

Sift together flour, baking powder, salt, baking soda and cinnamon. In a blender, process nuts to chop. Add to flour mixture. Process cereal in blender to fine crumbs. Add to flour mixture and stir. Process egg, sour cream, milk, oil and vanilla in blender, just until blended. Add apples and brown sugar. Process until smooth. Add all at once to dry ingredients. Add raisins. Stir just until moistened. Spread in a greased 8″ x 4″ loaf pan. Bake at 350° for 60 to 65 minutes or until toothpick inserted in center comes out clean. Let cook 15 minutes before removing from pan.

Lou Helen Yergat

Mission Viejo High School
Mission Viejo

Cranberry Bread

Makes 1 large loaf or 2 small loaves

2 cups flour
1 cup sugar
1½ teaspoons baking powder
½ teaspoon baking soda
1 teaspoon salt
juice and grated rind of one orange
2 tablespoons shortening

boiling water (enough to make ¾ cup;
    see below)
1 egg, well beaten
1 cup nuts, chopped
1 cup raw cranberries, halved
    (may use meat grinder)

Sift together the first five ingredients. Combine juice, rind, shortening and boiling water in a liquid measuring cup to equal ¾ cup. Add egg. Blend liquid into dry ingredients, stir only until moist. Add nuts and cranberries. Pour into a greased 8½" x 4½" x 3" pan. Bake at 350⁰ for 60 to 70 minutes. Cool, then serve.

Cari Sheridan   *Dexter Intermediate*
                                                                    Whittier

Pumpkin Bread

Makes two loaves

3-1/3 cups flour	1 cup salad oil
2 tablespoons baking soda	4 eggs
1½ teaspoons salt	¾ cup water
1 teaspoon cinnamon	2 cups pumpkin
1 teaspoon nutmeg or allspice	3 cups sugar

Sift all dry ingredients together. Add all other ingredients and mix until smooth. Pour into two greased loaf pans (9¼" x 5¼" x 2¾"). Bake 1½ hours in a 350⁰ oven.

Lillian Lee   *Hanford Joint Union High School*
                                                                    Hanford

Zucchini Bread

Makes 1 loaf

1 cup sugar	½ teaspoon baking soda
1 egg	¼ teaspoon baking powder
½ cup oil	1 teaspoon cinnamon
1 cup zucchini, grated	½ teaspoon nutmeg
1½ cups flour	¼ teaspoon lemon peel, grated
½ teaspoon salt	½ cup walnuts, chopped

Combine sugar, egg and oil and beat until smooth. Add zucchini and stir until smooth. Sift together flour, salt, soda, baking powder, cinnamon and nutmeg. Stir into zucchini mixture. Add lemon peel and walnuts. Pour into greased pan. Bake at 325⁰ for 60 to 65 minutes.

Lou Helen Yergat   *Mission Viejo High School*
                                                                Mission Viejo

Date Orange Cake

Makes 2 loaves

1 teaspoon baking soda	1 cup dates, cut up
½ pint sour cream	1 cup nuts, chopped
1 cup buttermilk	2 to 3 cups mixed candied fruit
½ pound butter or margarine	cut up and/or raisins
2 cups sugar	
3 eggs	**Topping:**
grated rind of 1 orange	Grated rind of 3 oranges
4 cups flour, sifted	juice of 2 oranges
1 teaspoon baking powder	1 cup sugar

Dissolve baking soda in sour cream and buttermilk. Set aside. Cream butter and sugar, add eggs and grated rind of 1 orange and beat thoroughly. Beat in flour, baking powder, dates, nuts, fruit and raisins. Lightly grease and flour 2 loaf pans, and pour batter evenly into them. Bake at 325º for 1 hour and 45 minutes.

While cake is baking, mix topping ingredients. Stir until sugar is dissolved. Spoon over top of cakes immediately upon taking them out of the oven.

Jan Neufeld   *Fullerton High School*
                                                                      Fullerton

Tart Cranberry Apple Pie

Serves 8

2 cups fresh cranberries	*¼ teaspoon salt*
5 to 6 large cooking apples, peeled	*¼ teaspoon nutmeg*
and thinly sliced	*Pastry for one two-crust 9" pie*
1¼ cups sugar	*1 tablespoon butter*
2 tablespoons flour	

Preheat oven to 425º.

In covered blender, blend cranberries just until chopped (about 2 seconds). In a large bowl, combine cranberries, apples, sugar, flour, salt and nutmeg; set aside.

Shape pastry into two balls. On a lightly floured surface, with lightly floured rolling pin, roll one ball into a circle ⅛" thick and use it to line a 9" pie plate. Spoon cranberry mixture into shell and dot with butter.

Roll remaining ball into circle ⅛" thick. Cut a few short slashes or a design in the center of the circle to allow steam to escape. Use this to make the top crust on pie.

Bake 45 minutes or until golden brown. (During the last 15 minutes of baking, place foil below shelf under pie to catch any drips. Serve warm or cool.

"Great change of pace, apple pie. Tart and flavorful."

Betty Ferber   *Rowland High School*
                                                                 Rowland Heights

Cranberry Cream Cheese Pie

Serves 8

Crust
14 squares graham crackers, crushed
¼ cup butter, melted

Filling
1 12-oz. package cream cheese
2 eggs, beaten
¾ cup sugar
2 teaspoons vanilla

Glaze
½ cup sour cream
2 tablespoons sugar
½ teaspoon vanilla
3 tablespoons sugar
1 tablespoon cornstarch

Fruit
1 1-pound can whole cranberry sauce

Crust
Combine cracker crumbs and butter thoroughly. Press onto sides and bottom of a 9" glass pie pan. Bake at 300º for 8 minutes.

Filling
Combine cream cheese, eggs, sugar, vanilla and beat until smooth and light in

texture. Pour filling into crumb crust. Bake in preheated oven at 300° for 40 minutes or until it no longer looks wet. Remove from oven and cool for 10 minutes.

Glaze
Blend together the sour cream, sugar and vanilla. Spread over pie and bake for an additional 5 minutes. Remove from oven and let cool.

Fruit
Blend cornstarch and sugar together. Gradually add the fruit. Bring to a boil and cook, stirring constantly, until mixture is thick, smooth and clear. Cool. Spread cooled fruit over cooled cheese pie. Refrigerate at least 5 hours before serving.

"Any fruit flavor works well, blueberry, raspberry, cherry, blackberry, etc."

Jeanette Gehrke   *Serrano High School, Phelan*

Delta Pumpkin Pie
Serves 6 to 8 (2 9″-pies)

3 eggs, beaten	1 tablespoon flour
3 cups pumpkin	1 teaspoon cinnamon
¼ cup molasses	½ teaspoon nutmeg
¼ cup maple syrup	¼ teaspoon cloves
1 cup brown sugar	1 teaspoon ginger
1 teaspoon salt	1 13-oz. can evaporated milk

Mix in order given in a large bowl. Pour into two 9″ pie shells. Cover edges of crusts with aluminum foil. Bake at 425° for 15 minutes, reduce heat to 350° and bake 45 minutes longer or until set. (Remove foil last 15 to 20 minutes.)

"The maple syrup is the secret ingredient!"

Linda Hubbs   *Lone Pine High School, Lone Pine*

Pecan Praline Pumpkin Pie
Serves 6 to 8

1 envelope unflavored gelatin	¾ teaspoon nutmeg
½ cup cold water	1 cup heavy cream, whipped
¾ cup brown sugar	¼ cup margarine
1 1-pound can pumpkin	½ cup brown sugar
¼ cup milk	1 cup pecans, coarsely chopped
½ teaspoon salt	1 baked 9″ pie shell
1 teaspoon cinnamon	whipped cream

Sprinkle gelatin over water in a saucepan. Place over low heat and stir until gelatin dissolves. Remove from heat and add brown sugar; stir until sugar dissolves.

In a bowl, mix pumpkin, milk, salt, cinnamon and nutmeg. Gradually blend in gelatin mixture and stir until smooth. Fold in whipped cream. Make praline crunch by melting butter, sugar and pecans and cook over moderate heat until mixture turns a golden brown. Remove from heat; turn onto foil. Cool and crumble over crust. Turn pumpkin mixture into shell and chill until firm. Garnish with whipped cream and serve.

Barbara Skiles   *Santana High School*
courtesy of Rebecca Wilke   *Santee*

Pumpkin Cheese Pie

Serves 8 to 10

1 8-oz. package cream cheese, softened
¾ cup sugar
1 teaspoon cinnamon
½ teaspoon cloves
½ teaspoon ginger
½ teaspoon nutmeg

½ teaspoon salt
3 eggs
1 16-oz. can pumpkin
1 teaspoon vanilla
1 9" pie crust, unbaked
pecan halves (optional)

Beat cream cheese until fluffy, gradually adding sugar combined with spices. Add eggs one at a time, beating well after each. Beat in pumpkin and vanilla. Pour into prepared shell. Bake in a preheated 350° oven for 40 minutes or until knife inserted in center comes out clean. During last 15 minutes of baking, pecan halves may be placed on top as decoration. Chill before serving.

Linda Leo   *La Sierra High School*
                                                        Riverside

Pumpkin Ice Cream Pie

Serves 6 to 8

1 baked pie shell
1 cup pumpkin
½ cup sugar
½ teaspoon salt
½ teaspoon cinnamon

¼ teaspoon nutmeg
⅛ teaspoon cloves
1 cup whipping cream
1 pint vanilla ice cream, softened

Mix together, pumpkin, sugar, salt, cinnamon, nutmeg and cloves. Fold whipped cream into pumpkin mixture. Spread bottom of baked pie shell with softened ice cream. Pour pumpkin cream mixture over ice cream. Freeze for at least 2 hours. Remove from freezer and let stand at room temperature for 5 minutes before serving. Garnish with whipped cream if desired.

Charla Rayl   *El Toro High School, El Toro*
Janet Van Wagoner   *Walnut High, Walnut*

Spicy Frozen Pumpkin Pie

Serves 16

2½ cups ginger snap crumbs
½ cup butter, melted
2 quarts vanilla ice cream, softened
1 can (1 pound) pumpkin
2/3 cup brown sugar

½ teaspoon salt
¼ teaspoon cloves
½ teaspoon ginger
1 teaspoon cinnamon
1 cup nuts, chopped

Combine ginger snap crumbs and melted butter. Press over bottom of two 9" pie pans.

Combine softened ice cream, pumpkin, brown sugar, salt and spices until thoroughly blended. Pour into pie pans. Sprinkle with chopped nuts. Cover and freeze.

"This is an interesting variation of pumpkin pie."

Mrs. Helen Stump   *Vina Danks Middle School*
                                                        Ontario

Christmas

Buche de Noel — Yule Log

Serves 10 to 12

2 tablespoons sifted flour
2 tablespoons sifted cornstarch
1/4 cup unsweetened dutch-type cocoa
1/8 teaspoon salt

4 eggs, separated
1/2 teaspoon vanilla
2/3 cup Mocha Butter Cream (below)

Preheat oven to 400°.

Grease and line a shallow 11" x 16" baking pan with waxed paper. Lightly dust with flour.

Sift together flour, cornstarch and cocoa; set aside. Beat four egg whites with salt until they hold soft peaks. Beat in sugar slowly, a tablespoon at a time, and continue beating until whites are very firm.

Break the four egg yolks with a fork. Add vanilla. Mix a spoonful of the egg whites with the yolks and blend well, then pour this mixture over the bowl of egg whites slowly. Sprinkle the cocoa/flour mixture on top and fold the entire mixture together gently. *DO NOT OVERMIX.*

Pour into pan spreading batter evenly. Bake for 10 minutes or until firm to the touch. Cool the cake a few minutes, then loosen sides, turn it out on a cake rack and peel off the paper. Spread thinly with 2/3 cup Mocha Butter Cream (below) and then spread with Whipped Cream Filling (below). Roll the cake into a 16" roll. Chill for one hour.

Spread the outside with the remaining butter cream. Use a fork to make the finish look barklike. Decorate with a sprig of cherry and tiny cardboard hatchet for Washington's Birthday or holly for Christmas.

Mocha Butter Cream
1 cup soft butter
2 egg yolks
4 tablespoons milk
1 teaspoon vanilla

12 oz. semi-sweet chocolate, melted
    and cooled
2 teaspoons instant coffee powder
    optional

Mix all thoroughly and follow above instructions.

Whipped Cream Filling
1 teaspoon unflavored gelatin
1 cup heavy cream, whipped

2 tablespoons sugar
1 teaspoon vanilla

Combine gelatin and 1½ teaspoons water in a small cup. Stir. Place cup over low heat for a few minutes until gelatin dissolves and looks clear. Beat cream in a chilled bowl. Add gelatin and sugar as cream thickens. Beat until stiff. Add vanilla. Refrigerate until needed.

Note:
To light log, place 2 cubes of sugar in aluminum foil. Place on back side of log. Pour orange extract over to soak sugar and light.

Libby Bruce

Troy High School
Fullerton

Cereal Christmas Trees

Makes 6 - 8 large trees or 16 - 20 small trees

3 tablespoons butter or margarine
32 large or 3 cups minature marshmallows
½ teaspoon vanilla

½ teaspoon green food color
4 cups Cheerios cereal
small gumdrops

In a large saucepan, heat butter and marshmellows over low heat, stirring constantly, until marshmellows are melted. Remove from heat; stir in vanilla and food color. Fold in cereal until evenly coated.

On waxed paper, quickly shape warm mixture with buttered hands into Christmas tree shapes, using about 2/3 cup mixture for each large tree or ¼ cup for each small tree. For ornaments, cut gumdrops into slices and press onto trees.

Cereal Christmas Balls
Shape mixture into balls, using about ½ cup mixture for each. Cut gumdrops into fourths and press onto balls. Makes 8 balls.

Lillian Lee   **Hanford Joint Union High School**
Hanford

Christmas Wreaths

Makes 18 to 20

½ cup butter
30 large marshmallows
1 teaspoon vanilla

4 drops green food coloring
3 cups cornflakes
red cinnamon candy

Place butter and marshmallows in top of double boiler. Cook until the marshmallows are melted. Stir until smooth and well blended. Stir in vanilla and food coloring. Fold in cornflakes. Drop by spoonfuls onto waxed paper and shape into wreaths. Add four or five cinnamon candies to each wreath for a look of holly.

Joanne Fial   **East Middle School**
Downey

Sugar Plum Christmas Tree

Makes 20 to 25 single small servings

2 3⅛-oz. packages vanilla pudding
    and pie filling mix
3 cups milk
1 teaspoon almond extract
1 cup water
½ cup butter or margarine

1 cup pancake and waffle mix
4 eggs
2 cups sugar
2/3 cup water
½ teaspoon cream of tartar

Prepare both packages pudding mix according to package directions, reducing milk to 3 cups. Stir in almond extract. Cover and chill (Filling may be stored up to 2 days in refrigerator.)

Bring 1 cup water and butter to a boil in a medium-sized sauce pan. Remove from heat. Add pancake mix all at once. Stir vigorously until mixture leaves sides of pan and forms a ball. Add eggs, one at a time, beating well after each addition. Drop batter by rounded teaspoonsful, about 2″ apart, onto ungreased cookie sheet. Bake at 375⁰ about 30 minutes or until golden brown. Cool completely on wire rack. Cut slit in side of each cream puff with small sharp knife and fill each by forcing almond creme filling into split through pastry tube or wax paper cone.

Combine sugar, 2/3 cup water and cream of tartar in a heavy 3 quart sauce pan. Cook over medium-high heat, stirring frequently to 315° or until syrup turns light golden brown. Using tongs, dip one side of each cream puff, one at a time, into hot caramel syrup. Form a solid circle on a serving plate or cake stand, using about 12 cream puffs. Continue dipping and stacking cream puffs in narrowing circles to form cone shape. Top with a single cream puff. Drizzle remaining syrup over stack of cream puffs. Decorate with candied fruit, if desired. Chill uncovered to set syrup. Refrigerate no longer than 24 hours before serving. To serve, cut and pull cream puffs apart with sharp knife and fork.

Sydney Fox   *Orange Glen High School*
                                                                      Escondido

Tree Trimmer Sugar Cookies

Makes 60

1¾ cups flour   1 cup sugar
¼ cup cornstarch   1 egg
1 teaspoon baking powder   ½ teaspoon vanilla
½ cup butter or margarine, softened   egg white

Mix flour, cornstarch and baking powder; set aside. Using electric mixer, cream butter and sugar until light and fluffy. Beat in egg and vanilla. Using a wooden spoon, gradually stir in flour mixture until blended. Cover, chill until firm enough to roll out.

On floured pastry cloth with stockinette-covered rolling pin, roll ¼ of the dough at a time to ⅛" thickness. Using 2" cookie cutters, cut in desired shapes. Brush with egg white and decorate with sugar sprinkles or decorate after baking. For tree ornaments, before baking, cut a ¼" wide hole about ¼" from top of each cookie.

Place ½" apart on a greased cookie sheet. Bake in preheated 350° oven 8 to 10 minutes or until edges are golden. Remove to rack to cool. Decorate with ornamental frosting and candies, if desired.

Frosting
1 egg white
¼ teaspoon cream of tartar
1¼ cups confectioners' sugar

In a small bowl at high speed, beat egg white with cream of tartar until frothy. Gradually beat in confectioners' sugar until thick and glossy.

Sydney Fox   *Orange Glen High School*
                                                                      Escondido

Vegetable Christmas Tree

Serves 10 to 12

1 large head cauliflower
1 large bunch broccoli
1 box cherry tomatoes

Clean and cut vegetables in bite size pieces. Use cauliflower as the tree and arrange on a plate. Outline it with the flower parts of the broccoli, and use the tomatoes to decorate the tree. The broccoli also makes the trunk of the tree.

Dip

1 pint sour cream
1 package Hidden Valley Ranch House Dressing

Combine in a bowl. Store in refrigerator 24 hours before serving.

Brenda Burke   *Mount Whitney High School*
Visalia

BV's Holiday Eggnog

Serves a group

20 eggs, separated
2 cups sugar
2 tablespoons vanilla
5½ pints half and half

2½ pints whipping cream
5½ cups bourbon
½ cup rum
dash of nutmeg

Beat egg yolks, sugar and vanilla together. Add cream and liquor. Beat egg whites until fluffy. Fold into eggnog mixture. Chill for 4 to 5 hours. Add nutmeg before serving.

Debbie Wilson   *Hueneme High School*
Oxnard

Friendship Tea

Makes 5 cups

1 cup instant Lipton tea
1 cup orange flavored Tang
1 cup granulated sugar

1 12-oz. package Wyler's imitation
  lemonade mix
1 teaspoon ground cloves
1½ teaspoon ground cinnamon

Mix all ingredients together. Store in Mason jars until ready to make. To make, mix 1 to 2 teaspoons per cup to individual taste with hot water.

"Delicious and everyone likes. Can be given for any occasion!"

Gage Jones   *South Pasadena High School*
South Pasadena

Hot Buttered Rum

Makes 32 drinks

Rum
1 pound butter
1 pound brown sugar
1 pound powdered sugar

2 teaspoons cinnamon
2 teaspoons nutmeg
1 quart vanilla ice cream

Combine all ingredients in a blender or use a mixer. Put 2 tablespoons of mixture in a cup, add 1 jigger of rum, fill cup with hot water and enjoy!

"Can be kept in refrigerator or freezer or placed in smaller containers and taken as a hostess gift during the holidays!"

Joyce Grohmann

Bellflower High School
Bellflower

Kahlua

Makes 2½ quarts

6 cups water
½ cup instant coffee
6 cups sugar

½ cup vanilla
½ gallon vodka

Bring to a boil water, instant coffee and sugar; then simmer for 2 hours. When cool, add vanilla and vodka. Serve.

"Drink and enjoy! I like to put the kahlua in empty Grolch beer bottles."

Cari Sheridan

Dexter Intermediate
Whittier

Ramos Fizz

Serves 4

3 oz. gin
½ cup sweet and sour mix
1 cup orange juice
¾ cup cream (half and half is okay)

1 egg white
1 tablespoon sugar
1 cup crushed ice
dash of nutmeg

Add all ingredients to a blender; add ice last. Whip up the Fizz and pour into wine type glasses. Shake nutmeg on top of each glassful

"Enjoy!"

Ginny Mohs

Vista View Elementary
Fountain Valley

Wassail

Makes 1 gallon

2 cups cranberry juice
2/3 cup sugar
7 cups water
¼ package cinnamon sticks
¼ package whole allspice

¼ package whole cloves
1 46-oz. can pineapple juice
1 6-oz. can Hawaiian Punch frozen
  concentrate
½ 6-oz. can orange juice frozen
  concentrate

Combine cranberry juice, sugar and water. Stir to dissolve sugar and heat to boiling. Tie spice into a cheesecloth bag. Add to the liquid and simmer 20 minutes. Remove spice bag.

Just before serving, add fruit juices. Serve steaming hot. (May be served from 30 cup electric coffee server.)

Willy Hall   *McPherson Junior High School*
                                                 Orange

Artichoke Dip

Serves 12 to 16 as an appetizer

1 cup mayonnaise
1 cup sharp cheddar cheese, shredded

1 7-oz. can green chilies, diced
1 8½-oz. can artichoke hearts,
  drained and quartered

Mix all ingredients. Bake at 350° for 40 minutes. Serve with Triscuits.

"This appetizer is very popular, and is usually one of the first to disappear at a party."

Shirley Wilcox   *Burbank High School*
                                                 Burbank

Party Cheese Ball

Serves a group

1 pound cream cheese, softened
½ pound sharp cheddar cheese, grated
¼ bell pepper, minced
¼ small onion, minced
1 teaspoon fresh lemon juice

2 teaspoons Worcestershire sauce
dash salt
dash pepper
1 small jar pimentos
pecans, chopped

Blend together the cream cheese, cheddar cheese, bell pepper, onion, lemon juice, Worcestershire sauce, salt and pepper. Add pimentos after other ingredients are thoroughly blended. Put in refrigerator to chill overnight.

Using your hands, form the mixture into a ball. Roll in chopped pecans. Serve with assorted crackers. (You could roll in chopped, fresh parsley.)

"I often give this as a gift for holiday parties. A friend took this recipe to England and Ireland, and it was a 'hit' with her relatives!"

Doris Oitzman   *Victor Valley High School*
                                                 Victorville
30

Cocktail Meatballs

Makes 5 dozen

1 pound ground beef
½ cup dry bread crumbs
1/3 cup minced onion
¼ cup milk
1 egg
1 tablespoon snipped parsley

1 teaspoon salt
⅛ teaspoon pepper
½ teaspoon Worcestershire sauce
¼ cup shortening
1 12-oz. bottle chili sauce
1 10-oz. jar grape jelly

Mix ground beef, bread crumbs, onion, milk, egg and next 4 ingredients; gently shape into 1″ balls. Melt shortening in large skillet; brown meatballs. Remove meat from skillet; pour off fat. Heat chili sauce and jelly in skillet, stirring constantly, until jelly is melted. Add meatballs and stir until thoroughly coated. Simmer uncovered 30 minutes. Serve.

Linda Troxell   *Thousand Oaks High School*
                                                                    Thousand Oaks

Dutch Babies

Serves 4

1/3 cup butter
4 eggs
1 cup milk

1 cup flour
4 tablespoons sour cream, cinnamon,
   honey or syrup for topping

Put butter in an 8″ souffle dish and put in the oven at 425⁰ until butter melts. While butter is melting, mix eggs in blender on high speed for 1 minute, then while blender is still running, pour in milk and gradually add flour. Continue blending for 30 seconds.

Remove pan from oven, pour batter into the hot, melted butter. Return pan to oven and bake until puffy and golden brown, about 20-25 minutes.

Lou Obermeyer   *Loma Vista Intermediate*
                                                                        Riverside

Mountain Mama's Mouthwatering Waffles

Makes 3 9″-Waffles

2 egg yolks
1¾ cups milk
½ cup cooking oil or
   melted shortening

1¾ cups all-purpose flour
1 tablespoon baking powder
½ teaspoon salt
2 egg whites

In a small mixing bowl, beat egg yolks with a fork. Beat in milk and cooking oil or melted shortening. In a large mixing bowl, stir together the flour, baking powder, and salt. Add egg mixture to flour mixture all at once. Stir mixture until blended but still slightly lumpy.

In small bowl, beat egg whites until stiff peaks form. Fold egg whites into egg/flour mixture. Do not overmix. Preheat waffle maker and lightly grease. Pour batter onto grids. Close cover of waffle maker. Cook until done.

"Delicious and tasty treat for hungry morning appetites. Serve with fresh fruit, ham or any favorite side dish."

Cheryl Ann Oravetz   *Hemet High School, Hemet* 31

Winter French Toast

Serves 6 to 8

2 tablespoons corn syrup
  (light or dark)
½ cup butter
1 cup brown sugar, packed
1 loaf white bread, unsliced
  crusts trimmed

5 eggs
1½ cups milk
1 teaspoon vanilla
¼ teaspoon salt

In a small saucepan, combine syrup, butter and brown sugar. Simmer until syrupy. Pour over bottom of a 9" x 13" dish.

Slice bread into 12 or 16 slices and place over sugar mixture in dish. Beat eggs, milk, vanilla and salt. Pour over bread. Cover and refrigerate overnight. Preheat oven to 350⁰ and bake uncovered for 45 minutes. Serve hot or warm or it will harden in the pan. (Can be reheated.)

Lou Obermeyer   *Loma Vista Intermediate*
                                   Riverside

Holiday Breakfast Casserole

Serves 8

1 12-oz. package hash brown potatoes
¼ cup butter, melted
1 cup diced ham or thin boiled ham
4 oz. Cheddar cheese, shredded
4 oz. Swiss or Jack cheese, shredded

2 eggs
½ cup milk
¼ teaspoon seasoned salt
1 4-oz. can diced green chilies, optional
Salsa to taste, optional

In a greased pie pan, spread hash brown potatoes. Brush with melted butter and bake at 425⁰ for 25 minutes.

Layer ham, cheeses and chilies on crust. Combine eggs, milk and salt and place on top of ham/cheese mixture. Bake at 350⁰ for 30 to 35 minutes. Place salsa on top when serving. This does very well when made in large quantities in larger pans.

"When you add the green chilies and red salsa, you will be ready for your Christmas breakfast. This recipe was given to the Home Ec Department by Barbie Whorton."

Marianne Traw   *Ball Junior High School*
                                   Anaheim

Christmas Jello Salad

Serves 8

1 6-oz. box cherry gelatin
2 cups boiling water
2 cups Coca-Cola
1 sliced banana

1 cup nuts, chopped
1 cup small marshmallows
1 small can crushed pineapple, drained
½ pint whipping cream

Dissolve gelatin in boiling water and add Cola. Let stand in refrigerator until almost firm. Add banana, nuts, marshmallows and pineapple; mix well. Whip cream. Stir into gelatin mixture. Chill until firm.

"Great for Valentine's too!"

Cheryl Sakahara   *Piute School, Lancaster*

Cranberry Souffle Salad

Serves 8 to 10

¾ cup sugar
¼ teaspoon ground allspice
2 cups water
2 cups cranberries
2 envelopes unflavored gelatin

½ cup mayonnaise
½ teaspoon shredded orange peel
1½ cups orange juice
½ cup pecans, chopped
Romaine lettuce leaves

Attach oiled foil to a 1 quart souffle dish and set aside. In a sauce pan, combine sugar, allspice and ½ cup of the water. Bring to a boil. Add cranberries and bring to a boil again. Reduce heat and simmer for 5 to 10 minutes uncovered, until skins pop. Cool to room temperature.

Soften gelatin in remaining 1½ cups water. Stir over low heat until gelatin is dissolved. Stir in orange peel and orange juice. Beat in mayonnaise until well blended. Chill until partially set (consistency of uneaten egg whites.)

Beat gelatin mixture with electric mixer for 2 to 3 minutes until fluffy. Chill until mixture mounds. Fold in cooled cranberries and the ½ cup nuts.

Meanwhile, line souffle dish with Romaine leaves, standing them upright around the sides of the dish. (Trim to fit if necessary.) Turn gelatin mixture into leaf lined dish. Chill 4 to 6 hours or overnight. (If chilling overnight, cover with plastic wrap.) To serve, remove collar and sprinkle with additional nuts.

"A very light accompaniment for a usually heavy holiday meal. The pink and green color add festive touch to your table as well."

Sandra Robertson

Whittier High School
Whittier

Holiday Gelatin Salad

Serves ?

1 6-oz. package cherry gelatin
4 cups water
1 bag (4-6 oz.) cinnamon red hots

2 apples, cored and chopped
¾ cup walnuts, chopped
1 cup celery, chopped or
   2 cups miniature marshmallows

Boil 2 cups of water. Add candy to water and stir constantly. Place gelatin in bowl; add boiling water with dissolved candy. Stir until gelatin is dissolved. Add 2 cups cold water. Stir. Chill until partially set. Add apples, walnuts, celery or marshmallows. Chill until set. Serve with poultry or ham.

"When marshmallows are added, it's more like a dessert; with celery, it's more like a salad."

Kathy Stowell

Rivera Junior High School
Merced

estive Frozen Fruit Salad

Serves 10 to 12

8 oz. cream cheese
2 tablespoons lemon juice
4 tablespoons sugar
6 tablespoons mayonnaise
1 pint whipping cream

1 small can fruit cocktail
2 bananas, sliced
1 small jar maraschino cherries
1 small can pineapple tidbits
1 4-oz. can mandarin oranges
parsley, for garnish

Soften cream cheese and mix with lemon juice, sugar and mayonnaise. Beat whipping cream and mix with cheese mixture.

Drain all fruits well and fold into whipped cream-cheese mixture. Pour into large mold. Refrigerate overnight. Unmold and garnish with parsley.

"Use large fancy jello mold. May be frozen."

Sylvia Kassap

**Paramount High School
Paramount**

Holly Green Salad

Serves 8

1 3-oz. package lemon gelatin
1 3-oz. package lime gelatin
2 cups boiling water
1 cup plain yogurt
1 cup celery, chopped
1 cup apple, chopped

½ cup nuts, finely chopped
1 15½-oz. can crushed pineapple
   with juice
1 large container small curd
   cottage cheese

Combine gelatin and boiling water, stir until gelatin dissolves. Add gelatin mixture slowly to yogurt and stir until smooth. Add remaining ingredients. Allow to set overnight. Compliments poultry or pork.

Susan Waterbury

**San Luis Obispo High School
San Luis Obispo**

Ribbon Salad

Makes 24 squares

1 6-oz. package lime gelatin
5 cups hot water
4 cups cold water
1 3-oz. package lemon gelatin
½ cup mini-marshmallows, cut up
1 cup pineapple juice

1 8-oz. cream cheese
1 1-pound 4-oz. can crushed
   pineapple
1 cup heavy cream, whipped
1 cup mayonnaise (or sour cream)
1 6-oz. package cherry gelatin

Dissolve lime gelatin in 2 cups hot water. Add 2 cups cold water. Pour into a 14" x 10" x 2" pan. Chill until partly set. Dissolve lemon gelatin in a double boiler in 1 cup hot water. Add marshmallows and stir to melt. Remove from heat. Add 1 cup pineapple juice (drained from can) and cream cheese. Beat until well blended and stir in pineapple. Cool slightly. Fold in whipping cream and mayonnaise. Chill until thickened. Pour over lime gelatin and chill until almost set. Dissolve cherry gelatin in 2 cups hot water. Add 2 cups cold water. Pour over center mixture. Chill until set.

34

"This also makes a beautiful molded salad, just reduce the amount of cold water for the top and bottom layers as package directions state.

"This salad is delightful for any occasion. Just change the flavor of gelatin to match the color scheme."

Mrs. Connie Willems   *Paulding Intermediate*
                                                          Arroyo Grande

Seven Layer Jello

Serves 12 to 16

6 packages unflavored gelatin   1 14-oz. can sweetened condensed
  (1½ boxes)   milk
4 3-oz. boxes flavored gelatin   9" x 13" pan sprayed well with PAM
  (each a different color and flavor)

Mix 1 box flavored gelatin with 1 package unflavored gelatin. Add 1 cup hot water. Dissolve and cool. Pour into pan and refrigerate until set.

Add 1 cup milk mixture (see below), and pour slowly over previous layer. Cover entire surface and refrigerate until set.

Repeat layer 1, using a second flavor of gelatin. Repeat layer 2. Repeat layer 1, using a third flavor of gelatin. Add remaining milk mixture. Repeat layer 1, using last flavor of gelatin. Cover tightly and refrigerate.

Milk Mixture
Mix 2 packages of unflavored gelatin with 1¼ cups very hot water and cool. Mix can of milk with additional cup of hot water and cool. Combine gelatin mix and milk mix.

"This recipe is particularly pretty cut in diamond shapes. It can be eaten with the fingers. Great for children!"

Patricia Wolfe   *Lakewood High, Retired*
                                                    Lakewood

Marinated Brussel Sprouts

Serves 4 to 6

24 brussel sprouts   ¼ teaspoon thyme
1 teaspoon prepared mustard   ¼ teaspoon pepper
1 teaspoon Worcestershire sauce   ¼ cup red wine vinegar
1 teaspoon sugar   1 cup salad oil
½ teaspoon salt   2 cups cherry tomatoes
½ teaspoon dry basil   ½ cup green onion

Trim ends of brussel sprouts. Slice each in half lengthwise. In a 3 or 4 quart pan, bring a large quantity of lightly salted water to boiling. Add brussel sprouts, and when water returns to boiling, reduce heat and simmer, uncovered, for about 7 minutes or until just tender crisp. Immediately turn into a colander and drain thoroughly.

Dressing
In a small bowl or jar, combine prepared mustard, Worcestershire sauce, sugar, salt, dry basil, thyme and pepper. Add red wine vinegar and salad oil and shake or stir to blend well.

Transfer *warm* brussel sprouts to a bowl and pour the mustard dressing, mixing to coat evenly. Cover and chill at least 4 hours or overnight.

Just before serving, add cherry tomatoes (cut in half lengthwise) and thinly sliced green onions to the brussel sprouts mixture, stirring gently to coat vegetables with dressing. Then using a slotted spoon, transfer the salad to a glass serving bowl.

Mary Lukan   *Boron Junior/Senior High School*
Boron

Company Baked Chicken

Serves 6 to 8

1 1-pound can whole boiled onions
3 to 3½ lb. frying chicken parts
¼ cup flour
¼ cup butter, melted
¼ pound mushrooms, sliced
onions to taste

¾ cup evaporated milk
1 10½-oz. can cream of mushroom soup
1 cup American cheese, grated
½ teaspoon salt
⅛ teaspoon pepper
dash paprika

Coat chicken with flour. Arrange in a single layer with skins down in melted butter in a 9″ x 13″ baking dish. Bake uncovered at 425⁰ for 30 minutes. Turn chicken, bake until brown (15 to 20 minutes longer or until tender). Remove from oven. Reduce heat to 325⁰.

Pour off excess fat and add onions and mushrooms. Combine evaporated milk, soup, cheese, salt and pepper. Pour over chicken and sprinkle with paprika. Cover with foil and return to the oven. Continue baking for 15 to 20 minutes.

"Nice served with rice as a rich sauce is created in the process and is delicious over it!"

Harriet Trousdale   *Roosevelt Junior High School*
Glendale

Chicken Normandie

Serves 6

3 whole chicken breasts, boned
   and split
12 shallots, finely minced
2 tablespoons butter
1 cup dry white wine
1 cup apple cider

½ cup apple brandy
1 cup heavy cream
salt and pepper to taste
3 tart cooking apples,
   cored and sliced
4 tablespoons butter

Pat chicken dry with paper towels and set aside.

In a skillet, saute shallots in 2 tablespoons butter until translucent, being careful not to brown. Add wine, cider and apple brandy. Reduce to ½ cup and then add heavy cream. Stir and simmer to reduce mixture until it coats a spoon. Salt and pepper to taste.

In a separate skillet, saute apples in a little oil, until just tender and then set aside.

In another skillet, saute chicken breasts in 4 tablespoons butter until done. Place on a serving platter and lay apple slices on top of each breast. Spoon sauce over each breast. Serve remainder in a sauce boat.

Shirley A. Wilcox   *Burbank High School*
Burbank

Saucy Tuna Bake

Serves 8 to 10

2 cups Bisquick
1 cup cheddar cheese, shredded
½ cup cold water
1 can tuna, drained
½ cup ripe olives, sliced

½ cup celery, chopped
¼ cup onions, chopped
¼ cup pimento, drained and diced
1 can condensed cream of celery soup
¼ cup milk

Heat oven to 425°. Grease square pan. Mix baking mix, ½ cup of the cheese and the water until soft dough forms. Beat vigorously, 20 strokes. Pat dough in pan, pressing up on sides.

Mix tuna, olives, celery, onion, pimento and ¼ cup of the soup. Spread over dough. Bake until edges are light brown, about 15 minutes.

Heat remaining soup, remaining ½ cup cheese and the milk over medium heat, stirring occasionally, until hot. Serve over top.

Esther Lehman   *James Monroe Junior High School*
                                                                        Ridgecrest

Norweigian Lefse

Serves 6 to 8

3 cups hot mashed potatoes
½ cup butter
1 tablespoon sugar

1 teaspoon salt
1½ cups flour, unsifted

Combine mashed potatoes and butter, stirring until butter is melted. Let cool, then add remaining ingredients; mix well. Shape into balls and chill.

Roll out on a slightly floured surface until very thin. Cook on preheated griddle or heavy frypan slowly at 375°, turning once to brown on both sides. Lefse will blister and brown in spots. Serve buttered or buttered with cinnamon and sugar.

"Made like a flour tortilla, but softer in texture."

Deanne Moody   *Monte Vista High School*
                                                                 Spring Valley

Chocolate Muffins

Serves 8 to 10

½ cup margarine or butter (1 cube)
1½ squares unsweetened chocolate
2 eggs
2/3 cup flour

1 cup sugar
1 teaspoon vanilla
½ cup chopped nuts

Melt together butter and chocolate in a double boiler. Beat eggs in a small dish. Mix flour and sugar together in a medium size bowl. Add the eggs to the mixture. Add the melted butter and chocolate and beat until smooth. Add vanilla and nuts. Fill paper-lined muffin pan ½ full. Bake at 350° for 15-20 minutes.

Fudge Topping
¼ cup margarine or butter (½ cube)
1 square unsweetened chocolate

2 cups sifted powdered sugar
cold strong instant coffee

37

Melt butter and chocolate together in a double boiler. Sift powdered sugar through a sieve onto waxed paper. Measure 2 cups and level. Add powdered sugar to the melted butter and chocolate in the pan. Remove pan from the double boiler. Mix ingredients well. Add cold coffee 1 teaspoon at a time until mixture is the consistency of thick, heavy fudge. Spoon fudge over muffins as soon as they come from the oven.

"Similar to brownies with fudge on top!"

Marilyn Wisely

Sparks Junior High School
La Puente

Amaretto Nut Bread

Makes 3-4 x 8" loaves

8 eggs, *separated*	½ cup *Amaretto*
3 cups *sugar*	4 teaspoons *vanilla*
1 pound butter, *softened*	1 cup *almonds, chopped*
3 cups *sifted flour*	

Beat egg whites until soft peaks form. Add 1 cup sugar gradually and beat until stiff peaks form. Set aside.

Cream butter with remaining 2 cups sugar. Add egg yolks, one at a time, beating well after each. Add flour in thirds, alternating with Amaretto. Mix well. Stir in vanilla and nuts. Fold in egg whites gently. Pour batter into greased loaf pans and bake at 350⁰ for 1 hour or until done.

"Melts in your mouth!"

Debbie Wilson

Hueneme High School
Oxnard

Bishop's Bread

Serves a group

3 eggs	1 cup *dates, chopped*
½ cup *sugar*	1 cup *nuts, chopped*
1 teaspoon *vanilla*	1 cup *whole candied cherries*
1½ cups *flour*	½ cup *mixed candied fruit*
1 teaspoon *salt*	3 tablespoons *brandy*
1 6-oz. *package semi-sweet chocolate chips*	

Preheat oven to 325⁰.

In a small bowl, beat eggs 5 minutes. Gradually add sugar and vanilla. In a large bowl, combine flour and salt. Mix in chocolate, dates, nuts, cherries, and fruit. Fold in egg mixture and spread in a greased and floured 9" x 5" x 3" loaf pan. Bake for 1 hour. Cool 10 minutes and invert. Poke 1½" holes and pour brandy over. Wrap tightly in foil and store at room temperature overnight. Slice and serve.

Netta S. Roberts

Wilson High School
Long Beach

Cherry Nut Bread

Makes 1 loaf

2 cups flour
1 teaspoon baking soda
½ teaspoon salt
¾ cup sugar
½ cup butter
2 eggs

1 teaspoon vanilla
1 cup buttermilk
1 cup walnuts, chopped
1 10-oz. jar maraschino cherries,
    drained and chopped

Grease a 9" x 5" x 3" loaf pan. Preheat oven to 350°.

In a mixing bowl, thoroughly stir together flour, soda and salt; set aside. In a large mixing bowl cream together sugar, butter, eggs, and vanilla until light and fluffy. Add flour mixture and buttermilk alternately to creamed mixture. Beat just until blended after each addition. Fold in nuts and cherries. Turn batter into prepared pan. Bake for 55 to 60 minutes. Remove from pan and cool on a wire rack.

"This is a very colorful quick bread to serve during the Christmas season."

Clyle Alt   ***Bell Gardens High School, Bell Gardens***

Gingerbread

Serves 6 to 8

2/3 cup hot water
1/3 cup shortening
1 cup molasses
2¼ cups flour
1½ teaspoons baking soda

½ teaspoon salt
1 teaspoon cinnamon
1 teaspoon ginger
½ teaspoon allspice
⅛ teaspoon cloves

Grease square cake pan.

Heat water. Add shortening to hot water and stir until melted. Stir in molasses. Measure flour, baking soda, salt, cinnamon, ginger, allspice and cloves into mixing bowl. Resift.

Add liquid ingredients to dry ingredients and mix well. Pour into greased pan. bake at 350° for 40 minutes or until top of gingerbread is light brown and springs back to the touch.

Terri Pratt   ***Sage School, Palmdale***

Strawberry Bread

Serves a group

1½ cups flour
½ teaspoon baking soda
½ teaspoon cinnamon
1 cup sugar
2 eggs, beaten

1 10-oz. package frozen strawberries
    defrosted with juice
¾ cup salad oil
¾ cup pecans, chopped

Sift together dry ingredients. Combine eggs, strawberries and oil. Add liquid ingredients to dry ingredients. Add pecans. Pour into well-greased loaf pan. Bake at 325° for 1 hour or until center tests done. Cool.

"Simple recipe. This can be made and frozen for gift giving during the Christmas holidays."

Betty Ann Lawson   ***Valencia High School, Placentia***

Eggnog Crown Cake

Makes 1 10"-Tube Cake
(12 large or 24 small slices)

2 tablespoons vegetable shortening
1¼ cups Quaker 100% Natural Cereal,
    original, crushed
1 cup butter or margarine
1½ cups sugar
4 eggs

3 cups all-purpose flour
½ teaspoon salt
½ teaspoon baking soda
½ teaspoon nutmeg
1 cup canned eggnog
1½ teaspoons rum extract

Generously grease a 10" tube pan with shortening. Pat 1 cup cereal onto sides and bottom of pan, letting large pieces fall to bottom. Beat together butter and sugar until light and fluffy. Add eggs one at a time, beating well after each addition. Add combined flour, salt, baking soda and nutmeg alternately with combined eggnog and rum extract, mixing well after each addition. Spoon into prepared pan and sprinkle with remaining cereal. Bake at 325⁰ for 1 hour and 10 minutes or until wooden pick inserted in center comes out clean. Cool 10 minutes and remove from pan. Cool right side up on wire rack.

Sydney Fox　　　　　　　　　　　　　　　　　　*Orange Glen High School*
Escondido

Fruited Pound Cake

Makes 5 small loaves

1 cup butter or margarine
1-2/3 cups granulated sugar
5 large eggs

2 cups all-purpose flour, sifted
1 pound glace fruit
¼ cup flour

Cream butter, add sugar and beat vigorously. Add eggs, one at a time, beating well after each addition. Add 2 cups flour, mix, then fruit and ¼ cup of flour. Mix well.

Line loaf pans (approximately 5½" x 3" x 2" or 5¼" x 2½" x 1⅛") with wax paper cut to fit the pan, and bake at 300⁰ for 1¼ hours. Cool. Wrap in plastic wrap to keep.

"Makes a nice light fruitcake!"

Ruth C. Findley　　　　　　　　　　　　　　*Antelope Valley High School*
Lancaster

Holiday Bundt Fruitcake

Serves 12 to 14

2 eggs
2 cups water
2 packages Quick Bread Mix
    (Pillsbury Date)

2-2/3 cups mincemeat
2 cups nuts
2 cups candied fruits

Put eggs and water in a bowl. Add remaining ingredients, stirring by hand until well mixed. Pour into greased Bundt pan and bake at 350⁰ for 80 to 90 minutes. Cool 15 minutes and remove from pan.

Patricia Jones　　　　　　　　　　　　　　　　*Norwalk High School*

Italian Christmas Cake

Serves 48

8 cups flour	1 package yeast
¼ cup whiskey	1 cup (approx.) salad oil
6 eggs	4 tablespoons cinnamon
½ cup shortening, melted	8 tablespoons sugar
1 cup sugar	2 pounds walnuts, chopped
1 teaspoon salt	2 pounds raisins
1 cup red wine	juice of 1 orange and grated rind

Make a well in the middle of flour and add whiskey, eggs, melted shortening, sugar, salt, wine and yeast (that has been dissolved in water).

Knead until mixture is dry. Divide into 4 parts. Roll each part into a ball. "Bless the balls." Roll each into a 10″ circle. Spread oil, cinnamon and sugar on dough with fingers. Sprinkle chopped nuts, raisins, orange juice (about 2 tablespoons) and rind over dough.

Roll dough into a tube (like a jelly roll) and turn tube into a circle. Secure ends with toothpicks. Bake on an ungreased cookie sheet at 300⁰ for 1½ hours. Keeps well in freezer for several months.

"This recipe was brought to the United States by my grandmother. Mary Urso from Saint Johns, Italy (20 miles south of Rome) in 1889."

Theresa M. Campbell   **Kennedy High School**
La Palma

Moist and Creamy Coconut Cake

Serves 12

1 package pudding included cake mix	2 cups Angel Flake Coconut
1½ cups milk	1 8-oz. container Cool Whip,
½ cup sugar	thawed

Prepare cake mix as directed on package; bake in a 9″ x 12″ pan. Cool 15 minutes, then poke holes down through cake with meat fork. Meanwhile, combine milk, sugar and ½ cup of the coconut in a saucepan. Bring to a boil. Reduce heat and simmer 1 minute. Carefully spoon over warm cake, allowing liquid to soak down through holes. Cool completely. Fold ½ cup of the coconut into whipped topping and spread over cake. Sprinkle with remaining coconut. Chill overnight. Store leftover cake in the refrigerator.

"For decorative touch, decorate top with towel-dried maraschino cherries!"

Shirley Rusche   **Norte Vista High School**
Riverside

Saint Nicholas Cake

Serves 10 to 12

1½ cups sifted flour
1½ teaspoons baking powder
½ teaspoon salt
3 eggs
1 cup sugar

1 6-oz. package chocolate chips
1 cup walnuts, chopped
1 cup dates, chopped
1 cup maraschino cherries, drained
    and chopped

Sift flour, baking powder and salt together and set aside in sifter.

In a large mixing bowl, beat the eggs until thick; gradually add sugar and beat well. Stir the chocolate chips, nuts, dates and cherries into the egg mixture. Sift in the flour and mix well.

Heat oven to 300°. Using a loaf pan, well-greased, line bottom and sides with waxed paper and grease again. Spread the cake mixture evenly in pan. Bake at 300° for 1 hour 45 minutes. Remove from pan at once and remove paper immediately. Cool on rack completely.

Next day, brush cake bottom, sides and top well with apple cider and wrap in foil. Store in a cool place for at least 10 days before serving.

Audrey Stock   *Sequoia Freshman, Fresno*

Bourbon Balls

Makes 6 dozen

⅛ pound butter (no substitutions)
1 pound powdered sugar
1/3 cup bourbon
¼ pound pecans

1 8-oz. package unsweetened
    chocolate squares
2 tablespoons butter
2 tablespoons paraffin

Mix butter and powdered sugar until like coarse corn meal. Add bourbon and mix with hands until smooth. Refrigerate for at least three hours. Take out dough and roll dough the size of walnuts around half of a pecan. Place in refrigerator overnight.

Place chocolate, butter and paraffin in double boiler over boiling water. Once it is all melted, turn heat down to low. Dip balls in chocolate mixture and place on wax paper. When set, place in an airtight container.

Antoinette De Neve   *Jones Junior High School*
Baldwin Park

Chinese Walnut

Serves 10 to 15

1 pound walnuts
1 cup sugar

peanut oil
salt

Boil walnuts in 6 cups water for 10 minutes. Drain in a collander, shaking to remove excess water. Sprinkle with sugar and toss until well coated. Spread out on a cookie sheet and dry overnight.

Heat ¼" oil in wok or skillet. Stir fry nuts until deep golden brown (sugar will caramelize). Spread out on a greased cookie sheet. Salt to taste. Store in covered containers or plastic bags.

"Be sure and give the recipe too; my guests always ask for it!"

Mincemeat Candies

Makes 6 dozen

1 9-oz. package condensed mincemeat,
    finely crumbled
¼ cup orange juice
¼ cup light corn syrup
¼ cup butter or margarine, melted

½ cup cornflakes crumbs
½ cup walnuts, chopped
½ cup dried apricots, finely chopped
1 cup walnuts, finely chopped
    (for coating)

In a large bowl, mix all ingredients except walnuts for coating, until well blended. Chill thoroughly. Shape into 1″ balls, roll in remaining nuts. Place on wax paper-lined baking sheets and refrigerate until firm. Store in tightly covered container in refrigerator. Makes about 6 dozen, about 40 calories each.

"For gift giving, use paper petit four cups!"

Ora Sharpe　　　　　　　*Franklin Junior High School, Long Beach*

Energy Bars

Makes 80 bars

2 cups Quaker Oats, old fashioned
2½ cups Rice Krispies
1 cup peanuts, unsalted
1 cup wheat germ
4 tablespoons margarine or butter

½ cup chunky peanut butter
1 10-oz. package miniature
    marshmallows
1 teaspoon vanilla
1 cup raisins

Heat oven to 250⁰. Grease a 9″ x 13″ oblong casserole dish or pan. In a roasting pan, warm the following ingredients: Quaker Oats, Rice Krispies, peanuts and wheat germ. In a large pan, melt the margarine, peanut butter, marshmallows and vanilla together. After the marshmallows are thoroughly melted, add the warmed ingredients and the raisins; mix thoroughly. (If you leave the pan over a very low flame, it will be easier to mix all ingredients.)

Quickly turn the mixture into the greased pan. Press the ingredients evenly with the back of a wooden spoon or the palms of your hands into the pan. Let cool completely. Cut into ½″ x 3″ bars. Wrap each bar in waxed paper and tie a ribbon to each end.

Astrid Curfman　　　　　　　*Newcomb Junior High School, Long Beach*

No-Bake Fruitcake Candy

Makes 2 large loaves or 5 small loaves

1 pound butter or margarine
1 pound marshmallows (large or small)
1 13-oz. box graham cracker crumbs

1 pound candied red cherries, halved
1 15-oz. box golden raisins
4 cups (1 pound) pecans, coarsely
    chopped

Melt butter in a large saucepan over low heat. Add marshmallows and stir until melted. Remove from heat and stir in remaining ingredients in the order listed. Press into 2 greased loaf pans (or 5 small 6¾″ x 3½″ x 2⅛″ disposable loaf pans) cover and freeze. Fruitcake will thaw in 4 to 5 hours. Unmold as you would a gelatin salad. Cut into slices and store in the refrigerator.

This candy is so sweet, you should cut into very small pieces. The small loaf pans are better.

"This recipe should be served as candy, instead of cake!"

Bonnie Shrock　　　　　　　*Kearny High School, San Diego*

My Creamiest White Holiday Fudge (Better than See's!)

Makes 24 pieces

2 cups sugar
½ cup evaporated milk and
½ cup water or 1 cup half
    and half
½ teaspoon salt
2 tablespoons butter

1 teaspoon vanilla
½ cup marshmallow creme, Kraft
½ cup walnuts or pecans, chopped
¼ cup candied cherries, cut in
    fourths, optional

In a heavy saucepan, combine sugar, milk, water and salt. Stir until dissolved. Brush sides with wet pastry brush to remove sugar crytals. Over medium heat, cook stirring to 236 degrees. Add butter and vanilla. Cool without moving (at room temperature) or stirring to 110 degrees. Beat until mixture holds its shape. Add marshmallow creme. Beat until thick. Add ½ cup chopped nuts and candied cherries. Spread into a buttered 8″ x 8″ square pan. Cool. Cut into 24 pieces.

Candied cherries can be marinated in rum or sherry for a few hours or days. Pat dry before adding.

"Great for people allergic to chocolate!"

Ms. Candice Rumenapp

Santa Monica High School
Santa Monica

No-Fail Fudge

Serves 50

4 cups sugar
20 marshmallows
1-1/3 cups evaporated milk
1 large package chocolate chips (2 cups)

1 teaspoon vanilla
1 cup nuts
1 cube margarine

In a large sauce pan, place sugar, marshmallows and evaporated milk. Cook about 7 to 10 minutes or to the soft ball stage. In a large bowl, place chocolate chips, vanilla, nuts and margarine. Pour cooked mixture over ingredients and stir until smooth. Pour into a buttered 9″ x 13″ pan. Cool and then cut into pieces.

Roberta Priestley

Alhambra High School
Alhambra

Velveeta Cheese Fudge

Makes 6½ pounds

4 pounds powdered sugar
1 cup cocoa powder
1 pound butter or margarine
    (do not use soft margarine)

1 pound Velveeta cheese
1 tablespoon vanilla
nuts, chopped (if desired)

Sift powdered sugar and cocoa powder together; set aside. Melt together, butter or margarine and Velveeta cheese. Pour melted mixture into sugar mixture. Mix well. Add vanilla and chopped nuts. Spoon into one 9″ x 13″ pan or two 8″ x 8″ pans.

Anne Stevens, School Secretary

Franklin Junior High School
Long Beach

44

Holiday Delight

Serves a group

3 cups granulated sugar	½ pound candied pineapple
1½ cups coffee cream	½ pound candied cherries
1 cup white corn syrup	½ pound pecan pieces
pinch of salt	½ pound walnuts, broken
1½ teaspoons vanilla	½ pound Brazil nuts, broken

Cook sugar, cream and syrup to soft ball stage (236°). Remove from heat; wipe edges of cooking pan down with a damp cloth. Add salt and beat until creamy. Add vanilla, fruit and nuts. Pour into greased loaf pan and press down. "Will keep well, provided you hide it away and bring it out when you wish it to be served! Otherwise, it's gone!"

"We've been using this recipe of Mrs. S.A. Kelly's for over forty years! It could be sliced ahead and stored in an airtight container. Super special!"

Mary Lou Sommer   *Monte Vista Junior High School*
Camarillo

Peanut Brittle

Makes 2 to 3 pounds

3 cups sugar	1 2"-square of butter
2 cups water	1 tablespoon baking soda
1 cup white Karo syrup	1 teaspoon salt
3 cups raw spanish peanuts	¼ pound coconut (optional)

In a six quart saucepan mix sugar, water and syrup. Cook to 325°, stirring constantly. Add peanuts and bring to 290°. Remove from heat. Add butter, baking soda and salt. Stir thoroughly. Add coconut if desired. Pour into a well-greased shallow pan and spread to about ¼" thickness. Cool, then break into pieces.

"Great recipe. Good and crunchy. May be stored in plastic bags."

Peggy Himenes   *Actis Junior High School*
Bakersfield

Peanut Butter Dreams

Makes 4 to 5 dozen

¼ pound butter or margarine	2 cups creamy peanut butter
1 pound powdered sugar	3 cups Rice Krispies

Mix butter, sugar, peanut butter and Rice Krispies together thoroughly. Roll into small balls and dip in chocolate topping (below). Refrigerate for several hours.

Topping
1 12-oz. package chocolate chips
4 tablespoons vegetable shortening
Melt chocolate chips and shortening in a double boiler. Coat the small balls in the chocolate mixture.

"This recipe is an excellent gift for the Christmas Holiday Season!"

Jeannie Burns   *Los Osos Junior High School*

Peanut Clusters

Makes 2 pounds

1 12-oz. package chocolate chips
1 12-oz. package Reese's Peanut Butter Chips
1 12-oz. can salted peanuts, without hulls

Melt chocolate chips and Reese's Peanut Butter Chips in the top of a double boiler. When melted, add the can of peanuts and blend together. Place by small spoonfuls on 2 cookie sheets covered with wax paper. Place in refrigerator to harden. Can be kept at room temperature in cool weather.

"Great for gift giving because they're so easy to make!"

Ann Farah   *Pioneer High School, Whittier*

Rocky Road Candy

Serves a group

1 12-oz. package chocolate chips
1 12-oz. package butterscotch chips
1 cup chunky peanut butter

1 10-oz. package miniature
   marshmallows
1 cup salted peanuts

Mix together chocolate chips, butterscotch chips, and chunky peanut butter and place in microwave until melted.

Add the marshmallows and peanuts. Mix. Spread the mixture in a greased 9" x 13" glass baking dish. Refrigerate until firm. Cut into squares.

"Great for gifts!"

Penny Putnam   *Divisadero Junior High School*
                                                                    Visalia

Sugared Nuts

Serves a group

3 cups walnut halves
1½ cups pecan halves
2 cups sugar

1 cup water
¼ teaspoon cinnamon

Mix all ingredients in a heavy skillet. Cook until water disappears and nuts have a sugary appearance. Remove from heat and pour nuts onto a baking sheet. Separate quickly with 2 forks.

"These nuts are quick, easy and enjoyed by all. They mail well, too!"

Madelyn V. Fielding   *Jordan High School, Long Beach*

Texas Pecan Logs

Makes 1 large 12" log

2 cups granulated sugar
1 cup brown sugar
⅛ teaspoon baking soda
1 cup evaporated milk or
   light cream
¼ cup corn syrup

2 tablespoons butter
¼ to ½ cup powdered sugar
1 package Kraft caramels
3 cups pecans, chopped (may take
   more or less depending on number
   of logs made.)

46

Recipe for "Holiday Chocolate Cake" on page 53 →

In a heavy saucepan, cook both sugars, baking soda, milk, and corn syrup. Cook on medium heat to soft ball stage. Remove from heat and add butter and allow to cool. Beat until creamy (mixture will begin to stiffen). Turn onto pastry board or marble slab dusted with powdered sugar. Knead until firm. (Depending on the weather, you may need to work in as much as ½ cup powdered sugar to make the mixture stiff.)

Shape into a roll about 1½" - 2" thick. Melt 1 package caramels with 2 tablespoons milk. Roll candy center in melted caramel. Then roll into chopped pecans. Press nuts firmly into candy. Wrap in wax paper and refrigerate. Can make 2 large logs or several smaller logs to give as gifts.

"My family's very favorite!"

Linda Hinson   Diegueno Junior High School
                                                                              Encinitas

English Toffee
Serves 16

unsalted crackers	1 cup chocolate chips
1 cup butter	walnuts, finely chopped
1 cup sugar	

Place foil in a 9" x 15" jelly roll pan or cookie sheet with 1" hanging over edges, folding edges up to prevent dripping.

Lay crackers side by side in pan. Melt butter, pour in sugar, and bring to a boil. Cook for 3 minutes stirring constantly. Spread mixture evenly over crackers. Place in 400° preheated oven for 6 minutes. Remove and sprinkle with chocolate chips. Spread until all are melted. Work quickly.

Sprinkle walnuts on top and place in freezer for 5 minutes. Remove and break into pieces.

Lucie Hymel   Washington Middle School
                                                                              La Habra

Jamoca Gingerbears
Makes about 1½ dozen

¼ cup vegetable oil	½ teaspoon ground cinnamon
¼ cup honey	¼ teaspoon ground cloves
½ cup molasses	¼ teaspoon ground nutmeg
½ cup water	½ cup chocolate chip "mini-morsels"
3½ cups all-purpose flour, sifted	¾ cup sliced toasted almonds
1¼ teaspoon ground ginger	1 quart Baskin-Robbins Chocolate Chip,
1 teaspoon baking soda	Jamoca, or Chocolate Almond Ice Cream

Combine oil, honey, molasses and water in a small mixing bowl. Sift flour, soda and spices together in large mixing bowl. Make a well in the center of the dry ingredients and add the oil mixture all at once. Stir until well mixed. Form into a ball and wrap well. Chill dough at least 1 hour.

Roll out chilled dough to ⅛" thickness on a lightly floured pastry cloth or board. Use a teddy-bear cookie cutter to cut out gingerbears. Transfer bears to a greased baking sheet. Decorate half of cookies with mini-chips for eyes and ears, and a moistened almond piece cut to approximate size for cookie mouth. Leave remaining cookies plain. Bake cookies at 350° for 10 minutes or until lightly

← Recipe for "Jamoca Gingerbears" on page 47

golden brown around the edges. Remove cookies to cooling rack. Once cool, freeze cookies for at least 20 minutes.

In the meantime, coarsely chop remaining mini-chips and toasted almonds. Allow ice cream to mellow slightly. Spread a 1" thick layer of ice cream on a plain cookie and top with a decorated cookie to create an ice cream sandwich. Smooth ice cream to conform to the cookie edges. Holding the sandwich gently, quickly roll edges in almond/chip mixture, pressing more mixture onto exposed edges. Freeze. (If the ice cream becomes too soft to work with at any time, return it and bears to the freezer.) Repeat with remaining gingerbears.

Baskin-Robbins Ice Cream   *Glendale, California*

Almond Snowcap Cookies

Makes 2½ dozen

¾ cup shortening	3 egg whites
¾ cup confectioner's sugar	¾ cup granulated sugar
1½ cups flour	½ cup flaked coconut
¾ cup raspberry jam	1 cup almonds, sliced

Heat oven to 350⁰. Cream shortening and confectioner's sugar. Blend in flour. Press evenly in bottom of an ungreased oblong pan (9" x 13" x 2"). Bake 12 to 15 minutes.

Spread jam over hot baked layer. Beat egg whites until foamy. Beat in granulated sugar, one tablespoon at a time. Continue beating until stiff and glossy. *Do not underbeat!* Fold in coconut and ½ cup of the almonds; spread over jam. Sprinkle with the remaining almonds. Bake 20 minutes longer. Cool. Cut into squares about 1½". Store in airtight container.

Patricia Smith   *Kern Valley High School*
Lake Isabella

Auntie Rhoda's Ginger Snaps

Makes 2 dozen

2 cups sifted flour	¾ cup shortening
1 teaspoon ginger	1 cup sugar
2 teaspoons baking soda	1 egg
1 teaspoon cinnamon	¼ cup molasses (Brer Rabbit green label)
½ teaspoon salt	

Sift dry ingredients twice. Cream shortening, sugar, egg and molasses. Add dry ingredients and mix well. Roll into small balls, then roll in granulated sugar. Bake at 350⁰ for 12 to 15 minutes or until tops are slightly cracked and light brown. They are soft to the touch and harden as they cool.

"A crunchy cookie. Great for dunking!"

Vicki A. Hansen   *Tranquillity Union High School*
Tranquillity

Candy Cane Cookies

Makes 4 dozen

½ cup butter, softened
½ cup shortening
1 cup powdered sugar
1 egg
1½ teaspoons almond extract

1 teaspoon vanilla
2½ cups flour
1 teaspoon salt
½ teaspoon red food coloring

Heat oven to 375º.

Mix butter, shortening, powdered sugar, egg and all flavorings. Blend in flour and salt. Divide dough in half. Mix red food coloring into one half of the dough. Shape 1 teaspoon of dough from each color into 4" ropes. (Roll on floured board to form rope.) Press top of ropes together and twist. Curve top of dough twist to form candy cane. Place on ungreased baking sheet. Bake 9 minutes or until very light brown.

"Besides being good for eating, they can be used as Christmas decorations, such as hanging them on the tree or tying them on packages — anywhere candy canes are used."

Karen Hay   *De Anza Middle School, Ventura*

Choco-Peppermint Cookies

Makes about 3 dozen

1 15-oz. package chocolate chip
    cookie mix
½ cup butter or margarine, softened

½ cup coarsely chopped nuts
1 egg
¼ cup crushed peppermint candy

Combine all ingredients; mix well. Drop by rounded teaspoonfuls onto ungreased cookie sheet and bake at 375º for about 10 minutes or until light golden brown. Cool 1 minute on cookie sheet; remove to wire cooling rack. Store in loosely covered container.

Sydney Fox   *Orange Glen High School, Escondido*

Yule Fruitcake Cookies

Makes 8 dozen

4 cups sifted flour
1 teaspoon baking soda
½ teaspoon salt
1 cup shortening
2 cups brown sugar, packed
2 eggs, well beaten

2/3 cup sour milk or buttermilk
2 cups dates, chopped
1 cup nuts, chopped
1 cup candied cherries, chopped
1 cup candied fruit and peel,
    (Radiant mix)

Sift together the flour, soda, and salt. Cream the shortening, add the sugar and eggs. Beat until light and fluffy. Add the sour milk and flour alternately. Then fold in the nuts and fruit. Chill the dough about one hour. Drop by teaspoonfuls about 2" apart on a lightly greased cookie sheet. Bake at 375º for 8 to 10 minutes or until set and lightly brown.

"They're yummy!"

Nancy Byrum   *Patrick Henry High School, San Diego*

Fruit Clusters

Makes 120

1 15-oz. package raisins
½ cup bourbon
¼ cup butter, softened
½ cup light brown sugar
2 eggs
1½ cups flour
1½ teaspoons baking soda

½ teaspoon nutmeg
1½ teaspoons cinnamon
½ teaspoon ground cloves
1 pound (4 cups) halved pecans
1 pound halved candied cherries
½ pound rainbow fruit mix

Soak raisins in bourbon at least one hour. Cream butter and gradually beat in sugar. Add eggs, one at a time, beating well after each. Mix flour with soda and spices and add to butter mixture. Add raisins with bourbon and remaining ingredients. Mix well and drop by teaspoonfuls on greased cookie sheets. Bake at 325° for about 12 to 15 minutes. Cool on racks and store in an airtight container. If possible, age for several weeks.

"Cookies are especially good with eggnog!

Susan Brown

Sowers Middle School
Huntington Beach

Fudge Peanut Butter Bars

Serves 12 or more

1 package yellow cake mix
1 cup peanut butter
½ cup butter or oleo
2 eggs
1 12-oz. package chocolate chips

1 can sweetened condensed milk
2 tablespoons butter
½ teaspoon salt
2 teaspoons vanilla
1 cup nuts, chopped

Combine cake mix, peanut butter, ½ cup butter, and eggs. Stir by hand until dough holds together. Press 2/3 of dough into bottom of ungreased 9" x 13" pan.

Filling
Mix chocolate chips, condensed milk, 2 tablespoons butter and salt in the top of a double boiler and melt over hot water. Stir in vanilla and nuts and spread over dough. Crumble reserved dough over filling and bake at 350° for 20 to 25 minutes or until light golden brown. Cool completely and cut into bars.

"Irrestible!"

Priscilla Bechok

Bell Gardens High School
Bell Gardens

Gumdrop Cookies

Makes about 3½ dozen

½ cup shortening
½ cup granulated sugar
½ cup brown sugar, firmly packed
1 egg, unbeaten
¾ teaspoon grated lemon rind
1 teaspoon vanilla
1 cup sifted flour
½ teaspoon salt

½ teaspoon baking soda
½ teaspoon baking powder
1 tablespoon water
1 cup rolled oats
½ cup coconut
¾ cup gum drops, finely cut with
    scissors
½ cup chopped nuts

Combine shortening, sugars, egg, lemon rind and vanilla. Beat thoroughly. Sift flour with salt, baking soda and baking powder. Add to shortening mixture. Then add water and mix well. Add oats, coconut, gum drops and nuts. Mix thoroughly. Shape into a roll about 2" in diameter. Roll in waxed paper and chill overnight. Remove paper, cut in slices about ¼" thick. Place on a greased baking sheet and bake at 375⁰ for 12 to 15 minutes. (If some cookies crumble while cutting, repress together.)

"This may well become your favorite Christmas cookie recipe!"

Shirley Rusche   *Norte Vista High School, Riverside*

Heavenly Holiday Chews

Makes about 4½ dozen

1 cup butter or margarine	½ cup all-purpose flour
1 cup firmly packed brown sugar	2 teaspoons cinnamon
1/3 cup maple syrup	1 6-oz. package semi-sweet
3 cups quick cooking oats, uncooked	chocolate pieces, melted
1 cup shredded or flaked coconut	walnut halves, 4 to 5 dozen
1 cup finely chopped walnuts	

Combine butter, sugar and syrup in heavy 3 quart sauce pan and bring to a boil over medium-high heat, stirring constantly. Remove from heat and add combined oats, coconut, chopped nuts, flour and cinnamon, mixing until well blended. Immediately drop mixture by level tablespoonfuls into medium-sized foil muffin cups. Place on cookie sheets. Bake at 350⁰ for 10 to 12 minutes or until bubbly and edges are light golden brown. Cool 10 minutes on cookie sheets.

Carefully peel off muffin cups, then cool completely on wire racks. Spoon ½ teaspoon chocolate onto center of each cookie, then gently press walnut half into chocolate. Chill to set chocolate. Store in tightly covered container at room temperature.

Sydney Fox   *Orange Glen High School, Escondido*

Fresh Orange Cookies

Serves a group

½ cup shortening	1 teaspoon baking powder
1 cup sugar	½ teaspoon salt
1 egg, beaten	2 cups flour
½ large orange, juice and grated rind	½ large orange, juice and grated
½ cup sour milk or buttermilk	rind
½ teaspoon baking soda	powdered sugar

Cream shortening and sugar. Add beaten egg, orange juice, grated rind, milk and baking soda. In a separate bowl, sift together baking powder and salt. Add to shortening mixture. Drop by teaspoonfuls onto greased cookie sheet. Bake at 350⁰ for 10 to 15 minutes. Remove. While slightly warm, ice cookies.

Icing
Sift powdered sugar and add to orange juice and grated rind until thick enough to spread.

"This is a very special cookie recipe. A family favorite for several generations!"

Patricia Wolfe   *Lakewood High School, Retired*
                                          Lakewood

Wendy's Apricot Horns

Makes 6 dozen

1 pound butter
1 pound cottage cheese
4 cups flour (if sticky, use more)
apricot preserves

2 egg whites
1 cup ground almonds
¾ cup sugar

Mix first three ingredients together and shape into walnut-size balls. Chill overnight. Roll each ball into a circle ⅛" thick and put on 1 teaspoon apricot preserves. Roll into a horn (cone).

Beat egg whites, then brush each cookie with the egg white and dip in a mixture of the ground almonds and sugar. Bake for 12 minutes at 375⁰. Cookies should be very lightly tanned around edges.

Emily Lewis, retired   **Cerritos High School, Cerritos**

Orange a L'Arabe

Serves 16

16 seedless naval oranges
water
1¼ cups sugar

1 vanilla bean, can be used
    several times
2 or 3 oz. Grand Marnier, or
    other orange flavored liqueur

Using a potato peeler, peel the skins from 8 of the oranges. Slice these thin peels as finely as you can. They should be no larger than toothpicks. Cover with water and bring to a boil in a saucepan. Drain and recover with cold water. Boil and drain. Cover a third time with cold water. Add the sugar and the vanilla bean and simmer the slivers until they become translucent and the liquid is syrupy. Set aside.

Using a long, thin, sharp knife, peel all of the skin from the oranges and the white underneath. Cut the oranges cross ways into slices ¼" thick. Pour the skin slivers (called julienne), syrup (but remove vanilla bean and save), and Grand Marnier over the orange slices. Cover and refrigerate.

"This is a very refreshing dessert. It can be prepared 24 hours in advance."

Eleanor Magorien   **El Toro High School, El Toro**

Holiday Surprise

Serves 6 6o 8

1 3-oz. package cherry gelatin
1 3-oz. package lime gelatin
1 3-oz. package lemon gelatin
2 cups pineapple juice

1 graham cracker crust
1 cup whipping cream
Pineapple and mint, as a
    garnish

Make cherry and lime gelatin according to directions on the packages. Make lemon gelatin with 2 cups pineapple juice (no water). Chill. Fold whipped cream into lemon gelatin. Dice cherry and lime gelatins and put into lemon mixture. Pour mixture into graham cracker crust. Let set 12 hours. Garnish with pineapple and mint.

"A pretty and tasty dessert!"

Holiday Chocolate Cake

Serves 10 to 12

2 cups sugar
1¾ cups unsifted all-purpose flour
¾ cup unsweetened cocoa powder
2 teaspoons baking soda
1 teaspoon baking powder
1 teaspoon salt
2 eggs
1 cup buttermilk or sour milk*

1 cup strong black coffee (or
    2 teaspoons instant coffee dissolved
    in 1 cup hot water)
½ cup vegetable oil
2 teaspoons vanilla
Ricotta Cheese Filling (recipe below)
Chocolate Whipped Cream Frosting
    (recipe below)
Vanilla Whipped Cream (recipe below)

Combined sugar, flour, cocoa, baking soda, baking powder and salt in large mixer bowl. Add eggs, buttermilk, coffee, oil and vanilla; beat at medium speed for 2 minutes (batter will be thin). Pour into two greased and floured 9″ layer pans. Bake at 350⁰ for 30 to 35 minutes or until cake tester inserted in center comes out clean. Cool 10 minutes; remove from pans. Cool completely. Wrap for freezing or set aside while preparing Ricotta Cheese Filling. Slice cake layers in half horizontally. Place bottom slice on serving plate; top with 1/3 filling. Alternate cake layers and filling ending with cake on top. Prepare Chocolate Whipped Cream; frost cake. Pipe with Vanilla Whipped Cream and candied or maraschino cherries, if desired.

*To sour milk: Use 1 tablespoon vinegar plus milk to equal 1 cup.

Ricotta Cheese Filling

1¾ cups (15 oz.) Ricotta cheese*
¼ cup sugar
3 tablespoons Grand Marnier, orange-
    flavored liqueur or orange juice
    concentrate, undiluted

¼ cup candied red or green cherries,
    coarsely chopped
1/3 cup semi-sweet chocolate Mini
    Chips

Combine Ricotta cheese, sugar and liqueur in mixing bowl; beat until smooth. Fold in candied fruit and Mini Chips.

*If Ricotta cheese is unavailable, substitute 1 cup heavy cream. Whip with sugar and liqueur until stiff.

Chocolate Whipped Cream
Combine 1/3 cup confectioners' sugar and 2 tablespoons unsweetened cocoa powder in small mixer bowl. Add 1 cup heavy cream and 1 teaspoon vanilla; beat until stiff peaks form.

Vanilla Whipped Cream
Combine ½ cup heavy cream, 2 tablespoons confectioners' sugar and ½ teaspoon vanilla in small mixer bowl; beat until stiff peaks form.

Hershey Foods Corporation (Photo on page 46)   **Hershey, PA**

Plum Duff

Serves 8

2 eggs
1 cup brown sugar
½ cup margarine, melted and hot
2 cups pitted prune, cooked
    and drained

1 cup flour
½ teaspoon salt
1 tablespoon milk
1 teaspoon baking soda
cherries, if desired

Beat eggs well. Stir in sugar, mixed with hot melted margarine. Blend in well drained prunes, flour and salt. In a separate bowl, dissolve milk and baking soda; add to prune mixture. Place in a well-buttered mold and steam for 1 to 1½ hours. Unmold on serving tray. Surround with holly leaves and garnish with cherries, if desired. Serve with sauce.

Pudding Sauce
¼ cup butter
1 cup brown sugar

2 egg whites
1 cup whipping cream

Melt butter and sugar in top of a double boiler. Beat egg whites and add to double boiler. Heat through, then cool. Whip cream and fold into cooled mixture.

Phyllis Kaylor

Ray Kroc Middle School
San Diego

English Trifle

Serves 10 to 12

1 loaf angel food cake, sliced ½"
    thick or 24 ladyfingers
½ cup cream sherry
1 small jar raspberry jam

pastry cream (see below)
whipping cream
1 package slivered almonds
10-12 maraschino cherries

The night before, slice cake and sprinkle with sherry. Cover lightly so it won't get stale. Let sit overnight to allow alcohol to evaporate.

The next day, spread raspberry jam on top of sherried cake layers (or ladyfingers). Layer bottom of a bowl with 1/3 of the cake and pour 1/3 of the pastry cream over the top. Sprinkle with nuts. Layer cake, cream and nuts in order until all ingredients are used. Top with whipped cream and garnish with maraschino cherries and slivered almonds. Refrigerate 1 to 2 hours before serving.

Pastry Cream
1-1/3 cups sugar
2/3 cup flour
¼ teaspoon salt
4 cups milk

10 egg yolks, well beaten
2 tablespoons butter
1 teaspoon vanilla

Mix sugar, flour and salt together in top of double boiler. Slowly add milk to form a smooth mixture. Cook over low medium heat stirring constantly until mixture begins to thicken. *Slowly* pour ½ of hot milk mixture into a bowl of the beaten egg yolks stirring constantly. Then pour all the mixture back into the double boiler and stir until thick. Add butter and vanilla. Chill.

*You can use 2 boxes of custard mix or 2 boxes of vanilla pudding mix, if desired. It's less expensive and not as rich!

Karen Spence

Trona High School
Trona

Trifle Pudding

Serves 16

1 3¼-oz. package vanilla pudding
    and pie filling mix (**not** instant)
2 cups half and half
2 tablespoons dark Puerto Rican Rum
3 tablespoons sugar
2 cups whipping cream

2 10"-round sponge cake layers
    (Angelfood or Chiffon)
¼ cup brandy
¼ cup dry sherry wine
30 to 38 whole strawberries
2 tablespoons red raspberry preserves

Combine pudding mix with half and half. Cook on temperature controlled top burner, using a low heat at 200⁰ for 12 to 15 minutes or until mixture comes to a boil and partially thickens. Stir well occasionally. Turn off heat and allow to cool slightly. Mix in rum. Chill pudding thoroughly. Whip 1¼ cups cream and 1 tablespoon sugar until stiff. Fold into chilled pudding mixture. Using a brush, coat a deep, 10" diameter bowl, with raspberry preserves to within 1" of top.

To Assemble

Slice both sponge cakes horizontally into halves. Skim crust off top of both layers. Place top slice, crust side up in bottom of preserves-coated bowl, curving outer edge of layer upward. Combine brandy and sherry, and sprinkle a fourth of the mixture (approximately 2 tablespoons) over the cake slice. Next, spread 1/3 of the chilled pudding mixture over the surface of the cake slice. Repeat procedure 2 additional times. Finish by arranging 15 to 18 strawberries on the top of the third layer of pudding and cover with fourth cake layer, crust side down. Sprinkle with remaining brandy-sherry mixture. Whip the remaining 1 cup cream and 2 tablespoons sugar until stiff. Make mounds of whipped cream around the edge of the bowl and across the diameter with a spoon. Top each mound with a strawberry. Refrigerate *at least* 2 hours.

"For faster preparation, use any non-dairy topping in place of whipping cream. Also this recipe is supposed to be the trifle served at the Five Crowns Restaurant in Laguna Beach!"

Diedre Simon

Norwalk High School
Norwalk

Blue Cheese Tart

Serves 12

1 pastry crust
2 3-oz. packages cream cheese
4 oz. blue cheese
2 tablespoons butter, softened
¼ cup heavy cream

3 eggs
⅛ teaspoon cayenne
¼ teaspoon salt
⅛ teaspoon pepper
1 teaspoon chives, chopped

Roll out pastry crust to a 12" round to fit a 9" fluted tart pan with a removable bottom.

Beat cream cheese until softened. Crumble in blue cheese; beat until blended. Add butter, cream, eggs and seasonings. Beat until smooth. Stir in chives. Pour into pastry-lined pan and bake at 375⁰ for 45 minutes. Cool 5 minutes on wire rack. Loosen and remove side of pan. Cut into 12 servings. Garnish with additional chopped chives.

Anna Atkin

Monache High School
Porterville

New Year's

Fruit Punch for a Crowd

Serves 50

1 cup water
2 cups sugar
1 cup strong hot tea
2 cups fruit syrup (strawberry
    or loganberry)
1 cup lemon juice

2 cups orange juice
2 cups pineapple juice
4 quarts ice water
1 cup maraschino cherries
1 quart soda water

Boil together 5 minutes 1 cup water and 2 cups sugar. Add tea, fruit syrup, lemon juice, orange juice and pineapple juice to sugar mixture. Let stand 30 minutes. Add ice water, maraschino cherries and soda water. Pour over ice in punch bowl.

"A ring mold of lemoned ice and mint is pretty in the punch bowl."

Vera Wilson   **Del Dios Middle School**
Escondido

Hot Spiced Wine

Serves 6 to 8

½ liter rose wine
½ gallon cranberry juice
1 quart apple juice

4 cinnamon sticks
½ teaspoon whole cloves
Orange or lemon slices

Place all ingredients in a crock pot. Cook on low for 5 hours. Top with sliced orange or lemons to serve.

Peggy Stevens   **Santa Ynez Valley High School**
Santa Ynez

Ginger Dip

Serves 8

1 cup chilled mayonnaise
1 cup sour cream
¼ cup onion, finely chopped
¼ cup watercress, finely chopped

1-2 tablespoons candied ginger,
    finely minced
2 cloves garlic, minced
1 tablespoon soy sauce
dash salt

Mix all ingredients together an keep chilled until serving time. Great served with raw vegetables.

Linda Hinson   **Diegueno Junior High School**
Encinitas

Pizza Fondue

Serves 6 to 8

¼ cup onion, chopped
½ pound ground beef
2 tablespoons margarine
2 10½-oz. cans pizza sauce
1 tablespoon cornstarch

1½ teaspoon fennel seed
1½ teaspoon oregano
¼ teaspoon garlic powder
1 cup cheddar cheese, grated
1 cup Mozzarella cheese, grated

Brown onion and meat in margarine in an electric fondue pot at high temperature. Reduce heat to medium. In a bowl, mix cornstarch and seasonings into the pizza sauce. Add to onion and meat mixture. Stir well. When mixture thickens and bubbles, add cheese by thirds, stirring well after each addition.

Serve with garlic bread cubes, toasted English muffin cubes, or serve over toasted English muffins.

Carole Delap   *Golden West High School*
                                                             Visalia

Sheepherder's Bread Fondue

Serves 15 to 20

1 loaf sourdough bread
  (round, unsliced is ideal)
1 8-oz. Riccotti cheese
1 8-oz. cream cheese
1 can crab (or frozen)
½ cup mayonnaise

2 teaspoons lemon juice
1 tablespoon Worcestershire
  sauce
6 green onions, thinly sliced
14 shakes garlic salt
14 shakes black pepper

Hollow out 1 loaf of sourdough bread, reserve pieces.

Mix together all ingredients and put into the hollowed bread. Wrap in foil and bake at 350⁰ for 1 hour 15 minutes. Remove and serve, using bread pieces as dippers.

"You can use fondue forks, chips or crackers with this dip, too!"

Nikki Van Camp   *Poly High School*
                                                             Riverside

Cheese Herb Pretzels

Makes 30

1 cup all-purpose flour, unsifted
½ cup butter or margarine
2 tablespoons grated Parmesian cheese
1 cup shredded sharp cheddar cheese
½ teaspoon garlic

½ teaspoon onion powder
¾ teaspoon Italian herbs (or use ¼
  teaspoon each dry basil, oregano,
  and rosemary leaves)
3 to 3½ tablespoons water

Combine flour and butter (cut in chunks) in bowl. With a pastry blender or two knives, cut in the butter until particles are no longer distinguishable. Stir in Parmesian and cheddar cheeses, garlic, onion powder, and herbs. Sprinkle water over the mixture, a tablespoon at a time, while you toss it lightly with a fork until moistened.

Gather dough up into a ball. Divide in half, then divide each portion into 12 equal pieces. If dough seems soft, wrap and chill until firm.

Roll pieces of dough with the palms of your hands on a very lightly floured board into thin 11″ ropes. Twist into pretzel shapes and place slightly apart on an ungreased baking sheet. Bake at 425⁰ for 12 to 15 minutes or until golden brown. Cool on wire racks. Wrap airtight and store. May be frozen and made ahead.

Brenda Burke   *Mount Whitney High School*
                                                             Visalia

Party Cheese Puffs

As an appetizer serves 12 to 15 people

1 loaf firm bread
½ cup butter
1 3-oz. package cream cheese

¼ pound sharp cheddar cheese
2 egg whites

Trim crust off the bread. Cut into 1" cubes. In a double boiler, melt butter and cheeses (or in a microwave). Beat egg whites until stiff. Add beaten egg whites to melted cheese mixture; stir. Dip bread cubes in cheese mixture and place on cookie sheets. Refrigerate for a few hours or overnight (can be frozen). Just before serving, bake at 400⁰ for 12 to 15 minutes until brown.

Esther Siville   *Ventura High School, Ventura*

Frosted Pimento Cheese Rolls Hors d'Oeuvres

Serves a group

1 tablespoon minced onion
2 tablespoons water
2 to 4 slices of bread
2 tablespoons mayonnaise

¼ to ½ cup American cheese, grated or shredded
2 tablespoons pimento
3 tablespoons chopped parsley or watercress

Stir onion into water and let stand 5 minutes. Trim crust off bread. Beat together butter, mayonnaise and cheese. Mix onion, pimento, watercress or parsley together and add to cheese mixture. Spread one side of each bread slice with cheese mixture, until you have used 2/3 of the total amount. Roll each like a jelly roll and place close together on a baking sheet. Spread tops with remaining cheese mixture. Just before serving, set into a moderately hot oven (350⁰ to 375⁰) until rolls are deep golden brown or about 10 to 12 minutes.

"This recipe can be increased and used for appetizers."

Myrna Swearingen   *Norco High School, Norco*

Pineapple Cheese Ball

Serves 12 to 24

2 8-oz. packages cream cheese
1 8½-oz. can crushed pineapple, drained
2 cups pecans or walnuts, chopped
¼ cup green pepper, chopped
2 tablespoons onion, chopped

1 tablespoon seasoned salt
Pineapple slices and maraschino cherries, if desired
Parsley for garnish, if desired

Soften cream cheese. gradually stir in crushed pineapple, 1 cup nuts, green pepper, onion and salt. Chill well. Form into a large ball or two smaller ones and roll in remaining 1 cup nuts. Wrap in plastic wrap and chill thoroughly. Garnish with twists of pineapple slices, maraschino cherries and parsley if desired. Serve with assorted crackers.

Note: *Vice Principal Joan Fuchs gave me this recipe a couple of years ago and I have used it for New Year's day snacking ever since. Try it, you'll like it!"*

Erma Jean Crider   *Sanger High School, Sanger* 59

Artichoke Fritatta

Makes 77 1" squares

2 6-oz. jars marinated artichoke
   hearts
1 small onion, minced
1 small clove garlic, minced
4 eggs
¼ cup dry bread crumbs

¼ teaspoon salt
⅛ teaspoon pepper
⅛ teaspoon oregano
⅛ teaspoon Tabasco
½ pound grated cheese
2 teaspoons minced parsley

Saute onion and garlic in marinade from one jar of artichoke hearts. Drain other jar and finely chop all artichokes. Beat eggs, add crumbs, salt and spices. Stir in cheese, artichokes and onion miniature. Pour into buttered 7" x 11" pan and bake at 325⁰ for 30 minutes or until set. Cool and cut for serving into 1" squares.

"Freezes well. May also be served as main course for luncheon."

Susie Pendleton

Cerritos High School
Cerritos

Hot Mushroom Turnovers

Makes 6 dozen

2 8-oz. packages cream cheese,
   softened
3 cups all-purpose flour
1 cup butter or margarine, softened
6 tablespoons butter or margarine
1 pound mushrooms, minced

1 large onion, minced
½ cup sour cream
2 teaspoons salt
½ teaspoon thyme leaves
4 tablespoons flour
1 egg, beaten

About 2 hours before serving:

In a large bowl with mixer at medium speed, beat cream cheese, flour and 1 cup butter or margarine until smooth. Shape into a ball, wrap, refrigerate 1 hour or overnight.

Meanwhile, in a 10" skillet over medium heat, melt 6 tablespoons butter or margarine, cook mushrooms and onion until tender, stirring occasionally. Stir in sour cream, salt, thyme, and flour; set aside.

On floured surface with floured rolling pin, roll ¼ of the dough to ⅛" thickness. With floured 2¾" cookie cutter, cut out as many circles as possible. Repeat until all dough is gone.

Preheat oven to 450⁰. Onto one half of each dough circle, place a teaspoon of mushroom mixture. Brush edges of circles with some egg and fold dough over filling. Make sure all the filling is tucked securely inside.

With a fork, firmly press edges together to seal, then prick tops. Place turnovers on an ungreased cookie sheet and brush with remaining egg. Bake at 450⁰ for 12 to 14 minutes, or until golden brown.

"Turnovers can be frozen unbaked. If so, bake 5 minutes longer. These are delicious and only 65 calories per turnover!"

Linda Hsieh

Alhambra High School
Alhambra

Zucchini Cheese Appetizers

Makes 5 dozen

⅛ cup salad oil
½ small onion, chopped
½ clove garlic, minced
1¼ cups zucchini, shredded
3 eggs, beaten
¼ cup dry fine bread crumbs
¼ teaspoon salt

¼ teaspoon basil
¼ teaspoon oregano leaves
⅛ teaspoon pepper
1½ cups cheddar cheese, shredded
¼ cup parmesian cheese, grated
⅛ cup toasted sesame seeds

In a frying pan, saute oil, onion and garlic; stirring until limp (about 4 minutes). Add zucchini and cook until tender-crisp (about 3 minutes). In a bowl, mix eggs with bread crumbs and seasonings. Add zucchini mixture and stir. Pour into a 9″ x 13″ pan for appetizers (or 8″ x 8″ pan for a main dish). Sprinkle with cheddar and parmesian cheeses and sesame seeds. Bake at 325⁰ for about 30 minutes or until set. Let cool at least 15 minutes. Cut into 1″ squares. Serve warm or cold.

Cathy Smith   *Lone Hill Intermediate, San Dimas*

Franks in Peanut Butter and Chutney

Makes 100 hors d'oeuvres

¾ cup smooth peanut butter
½ cup chutney
1½ cups chicken broth
3 tablespoons corn syrup

3 tablespoons soy sauce
2 crushed cloves garlic
2 pounds frankfurters

Cut each frank into five bite-sized pieces. Combine all ingredients in a large saucepan. Heat and stir constantly until very smooth. Add franks and continue stirring carefully until franks are covered with sauce. Reduce heat and continue to heat slowly until franks are hot. Serve from chafing dish with toothpicks.

"Fantastic flavor that gets better when reheated. Make ahead of party and freeze. Stores for months!"

Mary E. Richmond   *San Luis Obispo High School*
                                      San Luis Obispo

Clam Loaf Appetizer

Serves 6 to 8

1 large round loaf sourdough
   bread, unsliced
2 large cream cheese
2-3 cans minced clams
clam juice (save in can for later)
½ teaspoon salt

2 teaspoons lemon juice
2 teaspoons Worcestershire sauce
5 drops Tabasco
splash dried parsley
3-4 green onions, minced

Cut top off bread and hollow it out with your fingers, putting bread pieces in a bag for serving later. Mix together remaining ingredients in a bowl.

Fill loaf with mixture, put top on and wrap tightly in foil. Bake at 250⁰ for 3 hours. Serve, using bread pieces to dip into sauce.

"After the contents are gone, *eat the container!*"

Jeanne Koerner   *Rowland High School, Rowland Heights*

Antipasta

Serves 50

1 15-oz. can tomato puree
1 24-oz. bottle catsup
1 4-oz. can black olives, sliced
2 6-oz. cans small shrimp
1 small can mushrooms
1 can crab
1 jar artichokes, marinated

1 6-oz. can minced clams
   (and juice)
1 4-oz. can diced Ortega chilies
sugar to taste
vinegar to taste
garlic powder to taste
minced onion to taste

Open all the cans and jars, mix thoroughly. Cover tightly and chill. Serve with special cracker of your choice. Triscuits and Ritz are great.

"A very easy, elegant recipe everyone *loves!*"

Angie Garrett

Tenaya Middle School
Fresno

Mushroom Microwave Quiche

Serves 6

1 9"-deep dish pie crust, unbaked
1 teaspoon Worcestershire sauce
1 cup swiss cheese, grated
½ cup beef summer sausage, diced
1 teaspoon instant minced onion

1 4-oz. can sliced mushrooms, drained
3 eggs
1 cup heavy cream
½ teaspoon salt
1 3-oz. can French-fried onion

Using pastry brush, spread Worcestershire sauce on pie crust. Microwave on 100% power for 2 minutes, turn, microwave 2 more minutes. Sprinkle the cheese, sausage, minced onions and mushrooms evenly over crust. Beat together eggs, cream and salt and pour over filling. Sprinkle onions over top. Microwave, uncovered, at 50% power for 10 minutes, turn, microwave 7 to 9 minutes more or until center is set.

Rhonda Rohde

Warren High School
Downey

Vivian's Blackeyed Peas

Serves a group

1 quart blackeyed peas
6 cups boiling water

2 strips uncooked bacon or
1 beef bouillon cube
3 tablespoons corn oil

Bring water to a boil. Add peas and reduce heat to medium. Add bacon or bouillon cube, oil, salt and pepper to taste. Cook approximately 45 minutes. Serve.

"Eating blackeyed peas on New Year's Day insures a prosperous New Year!"

Vivian Pierce

"World's Best Mom"
Bradford, Tennessee

"Bowl Game" Monte Cristo Sandwich

Serves 6

18 slices bread
butter
6 thin slices turkey
6 thin slices ham
6 thin slices Swiss cheese

3 eggs
6 tablespoons milk
dash salt
pineapple slices (optional)
currant jelly (optional)

For each sandwich, butter 1 slice bread and cover with a slice of turkey. Top with a slice of ham. Cover with a second slice of buttered bread. Butter top of bread and cover with Swiss cheese. Close sandwich with third slice of bread, buttered side down. Cut sandwiches in halves and fasten with wooden toothpicks.

Beat eggs with milk and salt. Dip sandwiches in mixture and grill or saute in butter until brown on both sides or fry in deep fat, heated to 375°. Remove picks, serve with pineapple slices and current jelly.

"Great for after-the-game parties. You can assemble the sandwiches and make the egg mixture in advance, then dip and fry just before serving."

Marianne Estes   *La Mirada High School*
                                    La Mirada

"Super Bowl" Chili Soup

Serves 6

1 pound ground beef
1 cup onion, chopped
1 6-oz. can tomato paste
1 14½-oz. can stewed tomatoes
1½ cup water

2 15¼-oz. cans kidney beans
1 clove garlic, crushed
1 tablespoon chili powder
1 teaspoon salt
1 teaspoon cumin

Brown ground beef and onion in a large saucepan. Drain off excess fat, then stir in tomato paste and stewed tomatoes. Add water, beans, garlic, chili powder, salt and cumin. Cover and simmer 30 minutes. Makes 9 cups.

Anna Atkin   *Monache High School*
                                Porterville

Smokie Lentil Stew

Serves 5 to 6

½ pound of bacon
1 cup (6 oz.) lentils
1 16-oz. can tomatoes
½ cup celery, chopped
¼ cup onion, chopped
1 bay leaf

1 clove garlic, minced
2 tablespoons parsley flakes
¼ teaspoon pepper
1 teaspoon salt
1 teaspoon sugar
¾ pound package Smokie Links

Cut bacon into ½" pieces and place in large kettle. Cook, stirring occasionally. Add remaining ingredients except Smokie Links. Add about one quart water, cover and cook slowly one hour, or until lentils are tender. Add more water as necessary.

Meanwhile, cut Smokie Links into bite sized pieces. Add to bacon in kettle for the last 15 minutes of cooking.

"This hearty soup is great for tailgate picnics and for rainy days. It can be prepared ahead and reheated, making it handy for soup and sandwich meals in front of the television set on New Year's Day."

Clyle Alt   *Bell Gardens High School, Bell Gardens*

Sweet 'n Sour Chicken Wings

Serves a group

3 pounds chicken wings
garlic salt
cornstarch
2 to 3 eggs, beaten
oil
¾ cup sugar

1 tablespoon soy sauce
½ cup Japanese rice wine vinegar
4 tablespoons catsup
¼ cup chicken stock
1 teaspoon Accent
1 teaspoon salt

Cut wings at joints to make 3 sections. Cover tips with water and boil for stock. Discard tips after stock is made.

Sprinkle other 2 sections with garlic salt, roll in cornstarch, dip in beaten egg. Brown in hot oil and place in shallow baking dish. In a sauce pan, combine sugar, soy sauce, vinegar, catsup, chicken stock, Accent and salt. Heat until sugar melts. Pour over browned wing pieces. Bake at 350⁰ for 1 hour uncovered.

"Can be prepared ahead of time, then baked just before serving. These are so good, I've used them for a main dish! (Try to buy wings on sale and freeze until ready to use.)"

Carol Goddard   *Alhambra High School, Alhambra*

Sweet and Sour Pork

Serves 4 to 6

1 pound boneless pork
1 egg
1 teaspoon salt
¼ cup cornstarch
¼ cup flour
¼ cup chicken stock
oil for frying

Sauce
1 tablespoon oil
1 clove garlic
1 bell pepper, cut in squares
2 carrots, sliced
½ cup chicken stock
4 tablespoons sugar
4 tablespoons wine vinegar
1 tablespoon soy sauce
1 tablespoon cornstarch

Cut meat into ½" cubes. Make a batter of egg, salt, cornstarch, flour and ¼ cup stock. Dip meat in butter and fry in 350⁰ oil. Keep pieces separate. When puffed and golden, remove pieces of pork with a slotted spoon and drain on paper towels. Set aside while you make the sauce.

Stir fry in oil, garlic, bell pepper squares, sliced carrots for 2 to 5 minutes. Add ½ cup stock and simmer 2 to 3 minutes. Stir sugar, wine vinegar, soy sauce and cornstarch together, then add to the vegetables and cook until it thickens. **Now,** fold the pork pieces into the sauce.

"This is super when it is 'year of the dragon' and equally delicious when it is 'year of the mouse.'!"

Gwenn Jensen   *Mira Mesa High School, San Diego*

Poertzelki (New Year's Cookie)

Makes 3 dozen

1¼ cups water, warm
1 tablespoon yeast
2 tablespoons sugar
4 cups flour
4 eggs, slightly beaten

¼ cup margarine
2½ teaspoons salt
½ cup milk
3 cups raisins

Dissolve yeast in warm water (110°), add sugar and 2 cups flour. Mix and let rise about 1 hour, then add remaining ingredients. Mix. Let rise again 1 hour, then drop from tablespoon in hot deep fat and cook until brown on both sides. Cookie usually flips over when done on first side. Be sure fat isn't too hot or your cookie may be raw inside when dark on the outside. You may sprinkle with granulated or powdered sugar if desired.

"Family and ethnic tradition. We've had poertzelki served only at New Year's. It's a very special treat."

Carol Friesen

Tehipite Middle School
Fresno

Tina's Whoopie Pies

Makes 45 to 50 pies

2 cups sugar
½ cup Crisco shortening
½ cup butter
4½ cups flour
2 eggs plus 2 egg yokes
1 cup cocoa

2 teaspoons baking soda
2 teaspoons salt
2 teaspoons vanilla
1 cup sour milk (1 cup milk with 1
    tablespoon vinegar or lemon juice)
1 cup boiling water

Mix as you would a cake. Drop by teaspoonsful on a greased cookie sheet. (Grease after each batch.) Bake at 375° for 7 to 10 minutes.

Filling
4 egg whites, beaten until stiff
4 cups powdered sugar
8 tablespoons flour
8 tablespoons milk

1 cup Crisco shortening
1 cup butter
4 teaspoons vanilla

Beat with electric beater until thick and fluffy, 10 to 15 minutes. Spread filling mixture on a cookie and top with another cookie to form "whoppie pie." Wrap individually in saran wrap. Best if refrigerated or frozen.

Linda Tsutsui

Hanford High School
Hanford

Milky Way Bars

Serves a crowd!

1 box German chocolate cake mix
1 stick margarine, melted
1 can evaporated skimmed milk

2 eggs
1 15-oz. bag caramels
1 12-oz. package chocolate chips

In a bowl, combine the cake mix, margarine, half of the milk and all of the eggs. Beat approximately four minutes at medium speed with a mixer. Spread half of the mixture in a greased 9" x 13" pan. Bake at 350⁰ for 5 minutes. Remove from oven.

Either in a microwave oven or in a double boiler, melt caramels with the rest of the milk. Carefully spread caramel mixture over the baked crust. Then sprinkle with the chocolate chips. Carefully spread the rest of the cake mixture on top and bake at 350⁰ for 20 minutes. Store in refrigerator.

"These bars are very rich and delicious. A little goes a long way, and are best when served cold!"

Nancy Horn

Selma High School
Selma

Harriet's Chocolate Cake

Serves 8 to 10

4 squares unsweetened chocolate
½ pound butter
2 cups sugar
4 eggs
1½ cups cake flour

4 level teaspoons baking powder
½ cup milk
½ cup sour cream
2 teaspoons vanilla

Melt chocolate and butter together in saucepan; set aside. In a bowl, mix sugar and eggs; set aside. Sift flour once, measure, remove excess and sift twice more with the baking powder. Blend together, milk and sour cream. Add liquid and dry ingredients alternately, in thirds, to sugar and eggs. Add vanilla to chocolate mixture, then combine with dry ingredients.

Grease lightly a 12" x 8" x 1½" glass Pyrex pan and line with wax paper. Bake at 325⁰ for 45 to 55 minutes. Remove from pan as soon as possible. Let cool on rack (upside down).

Fudge Icing

4 squares unsweetened chocolate,
   melted
2½ tablespoons butter

5 tablespoons milk
1 teaspoon vanilla
1½ cups powdered sugar

Mix together melted chocolate, butter and milk. When slightly cool, add 1 teaspoon vanilla. Blend in powdered sugar and beat a little by hand with a spoon until right consistency for spreading. (If too thick, add a little milk. If too thin, add a little powdered sugar.)

"Freezing this cake makes it extra fudgey!"

Harriet Rivkin

Home Economist
Montreal, Canada

Valentine's Day

Berry Punch

Makes 2½ quarts

crushed ice
1 6-oz. can frozen lemonade
1 6-oz. can frozen orange juice
5 cups water

2/3 cup grenadine syrup
1 quart gingerale
orange slices

Combine juice, water and grenadine and mix well. Add gingerale. Pour over crushed ice in punch bowl. Float orange slices.

Gage Jones   *South Pasadena High School, South Pasadena*

Strawberry Slush

Makes 1½ gallons

3 packages strawberry Kool-Aid Mix
3 cups sugar
12 cups water

1 large can frozen orange juice concentrate
½ large bottle Hawaiian Punch
2 bananas, mashed

Combine all ingredients, freeze in milk cartons for 1½ to 2 hours or overnight. Thaw to slush and add 2 quarts gingerale or 7UP

Mrs. Sally Oxford   *Monache High School, Porterville*

Hello Dollies

Makes 24 squares

1 cube butter
1 cup vanilla wafers, finely crushed
1 cup chocolate chips

1 cup walnuts
1 cup coconut, flaked
1 small can sweetened condensed milk

Melt butter in a 9″ x 13″ pan and sprinkle the wafers over the top evenly. Sprinkle the chocolate chips, coconut and walnuts on top. Pour the milk over all and bake at 350⁰ for 30 minutes. Cut into squares while warm.

Francine Miller   *Upland Junior High School, Upland*

Strawberry Bread

Makes 2 loaves

3 cups flour
1 teaspoon baking soda
1 teaspoon cinnamon
1 teaspoon salt
2 cups sugar

2 10-oz. packages frozen
    strawberries, thawed
1¼ cups oil
4 eggs, beaten
1 teaspoon red food coloring
1 cup walnuts, chopped

Mix the flour, baking soda, cinnamon, salt and sugar in a large bowl. Make a well in the center. Drain the strawberries. Add the strawberries, oil, beaten eggs and food coloring to the dry ingredients. Mix well. Add chopped walnuts, if desired. Mix again. Pour into 2 greased and floured bread pans. Bake at 350⁰ for 1 hour. Remove from pan and cool.

Colleen Nelson   *Roosevelt Junior High School*
                                          Selma

Miniature Cheese Cakes

Serves a group

3 8-oz. packages cream cheese
2/3 cup sugar
3 eggs
1 teaspoon vanilla

Vanilla Wafers, crushed
Cupcake papers
1 can cherry pie filling

Mix first four ingredients together well. Line paper cup with vanilla wafers and pour mixture into cup until 2/3 full. Bake at 350° for 15 to 18 minutes. Remove from oven and cool. Top with cherry pie filling. Serve.

Jean Moore   *La Habra High School, La Habra*

Valentine Cake

Serves 6

1 3-oz. package cherry gelatin
1 cup boiling water
1 pint vanilla ice cream
1 small can crushed pineapple

1 small angelfood cake
½ pint heavy cream, whipped
few red candy hearts or sprinkles
  optional

Dissolve gelatin in boiling water. Add ice cream a spoonful at a time and stir until melted and smooth. Add *undrained* pineapple. Line bottom of loaf pan with wax paper. Tear angelfood cake into small pieces and arrange in even layer about 1" thick in bottom of pan. Pour in gelatin mixture and chill until firm. Unmold on serving plate and frost entire surface with whipped cream. Sprinkle with a few red candy hearts, if desired.

Joan Allan   *Los Cerritos Intermediate School*
Thousand Oaks

Heart Cake

Serves 10 to 12

½ cup butter
1½ cups sugar
1½ teaspoons vanilla
2 eggs
2¼ cups cake flour
3 teaspoons baking powder

1 teaspoon salt
1 cup milk
1 can ready-to-spread white frosting
red food coloring
red cinnamon candies

Preheat oven to 350°. Grease and flour one 8" square cake pan and one 8" round pan. In a large bowl, using electric mixer, cream butter and sugar until light and fluffy. Blend in vanilla. Beat in eggs, one at a time, beating well after each addition. Sift flour with baking powder and salt. On low speed, blend flour mixture into creamed mixture alternately with milk. Pour equal amounts of batter into prepared pans. Bake for 25 to 30 minutes or until wooden toothpick inserted in center comes out clean. Cool in pans on wire racks for 10 minutes. Remove from pans and cool completely.

To make heart-shaped cake, place square cake on tray with point toward you. Cut round layer in half. Place each half with cut edge against top sides of the square cake to form a heart. Tint frosting pink with a few drops of red food coloring. Frost cake and decorate around the edge with red cinnamon candies.

Joanne Fial   *East Middle School, Downey*

Chocolate Cherry Valentine Tort

Serves a group

2 eggs, separated
½ cup sugar
1¼ cups unsifted all-purpose flour
1 cup sugar
½ cup unsweetened cocoa
¾ teaspoon baking soda
½ teaspoon salt

½ cup vegetable oil
1 cup buttermilk or sour milk*
Cream Filling (recipe below)
Chocolate Whipped Cream Frosting
  (recipe below)
2 cups (21-oz. can) cherry pie filling

*To sour milk: use 1 tablespoon vinegar plus milk to equal 1 cup.

Beat egg whites in small mixer bowl until foamy; gradually beat in ½ cup sugar until stiff peaks form. Set aside.

Combine flour, 1 cup sugar, cocoa, baking soda and salt in large mixer bowl. Add oil, buttermilk or sour milk and egg yolks; beat until smooth. Gently fold egg whites into batter.

Grease and flour two heart-shaped cake pans or 9" layer pans; pour about 1-2/3 cups batter into each pan. (Reserve remaining batter in refrigerator while first 2 layers bake.) Bake at 350° for 18 to 20 minutes or until cake springs back when lightly touched in center. Cool 5 minutes; invert onto wire rack. Bake remaining layer; cool completely. Prepare Cream Filling.

Place 1 layer on serving plate; pipe or spoon 1" edge ½" thick around layer; spread ½ cherry filling in center. Top with second layer. Spread with ½ remaining Cream Filling. Top with third layer. Spoon remaining cherry filling onto top of cake, leaving 1" edge. Prepare Chocolate Whipped Cream.

Frost sides of cake with Chocolate Whipped Cream. Pipe top edge with remaining Cream Filling. Chill completely; store in refrigerator until serving.

Cream Filling
Whip 1 cup heavy cream with 2 tablespoons sugar and 1 teaspoon vanilla in small mixer bowl until stiff peaks form.

Chocolate Whipped Cream
Combine ½ cup sugar and ¼ cup unsweetened cocoa in small mixer bowl. Add 1 cup heavy cream and 1 teaspoon vanilla; beat on low speed to combine. Beat on medium speed until stiff peaks form.

Hershey Foods Corporation   *Hershey, PA*

Chocolate Kiss Mousse

Serves 4

1½ cups miniature or 15 regular
  marshmallows
1/2 cup milk
2 teaspoons Kirsch or ¼ teaspoon almond
  extract

6 to 7 drops red food color
1/3 milk chocolate kisses, unwrapped
1 cup heavy cream
4 milk chocolate kisses for garnish
  optional

Recipe for "Chocolate Cherry Valentine Tort" on page 72 →
Recipe for "Chocolate Kiss Mousse" on page 70 →

Combine marshmallows and milk in small saucepan. Stir constantly over low heat until marshmallows are melted and mixture is smooth. Remove from heat. Pour 1/3 cup marshmallow mixture into medium bowl; blend in Kirsch or almond extract and food color. Set aside.

Add 36 milk chocolate kisses to the remaining marshmallow mixture; return to low heat and stir until kisses are melted. Remove from heat; cool to room temperature.

Whip cream until stiff; fold 1 cup into chocolate mixture. Gradually fold remaining whipped cream into almond mixture. Fill parfait glasses about ¾ full with chocolate mixture; top with almond cream. Chill for 3 to 4 hours or until set. Garnish with a kiss, if desired.

Hershey Foods Corporation   *Hershey, PA*

Strawberry Cake

Serves 8

1 box white cake mix	2 tablespoons flour
1 10-oz. frozen strawberries	¾ cup oil
1 3-oz. package strawberry gelatin	whipped cream
1 cup nuts, chopped	red food coloring

Combine cake mix, strawberries, gelatin, nuts, flour and oil; beat well. Pour into an angel food cake pan and bake at 350⁰ for 45 minutes or until cake tests done.

Serve with sweetened whipped cream slightly tinted pink.

Mrs. Shirley Rusche   *Norte Vista High School, Riverside*

Valentine Jelly Roll

Serves 8 to 10

4 eggs	¾ cup granulated sugar
¾ cup sifted cake flour	1 teaspoon vanilla
¾ teaspoon baking powder	Powdered sugar
¼ teaspoon salt	1 cup tart jelly or jam

About 1 hour ahead, set out eggs. Preheat oven to 400⁰. Line the bottom of a greased 10" x 15", jelly roll pan with wax paper. Sift flour, baking powder, salt. In electric mixer, beat eggs until foamy. Beat rapidly, adding sugar slowly; continue beating until very thick and light colored. With rubber spatula or spoon, fold in flour mixture and vanilla. Turn into prepared pan, spreading batter evenly. Bake 10 to 13 minutes, or until light brown. Should bounce back when lightly touched with finger.

Lightly dust a clean dish towel with powdered sugar. When cake is done, loosen it from sides of pan; invert onto towel. Lift off pan and carefully peel off paper. Roll up cake very gently, from narrow end, rolling towel up in it. Cool about 10 minutes.

Unroll so cake will be on towel. Spread cake with jelly to within ¼" of edges. Start rolling up cake from narrow end by folding edge of cake over, then tucking it under; continue rolling cake, lifting towel higher and higher with one hand as you guide roll with other hand. Finish with open end of cake on underside.

Finish cooling jelly roll on cake rack. Sprinkle with more powdered sugar. Serve, cut into 1" crosswise slices, just as is or topped with vanilla ice cream.

Lenore D. Lee   *Monrovia High School, Monrovia*

← Recipe for "Killarney Chocolate Pie" on page 78
← Recipe for "Shamrock Chocolate Cookies" on page 79
← Recipe for "Irish Hot Chocolate" on page 79

Brownie Valentine Cookie

Makes 2 Big Cookies

4 oz. unsweetened chocolate
2/3 cup margarine
2 cups sugar
4 eggs
1 teaspoon vanilla

1½ cups flour
1 teaspoon baking powder
¾ teaspoon salt
1 cup walnuts, chopped

Grease 2 heart-shaped cake pans. Line bottoms with waxed paper, then grease paper.

In a small saucepan, stir 4 squares (4 oz.) unsweetened chocolate with margarine over low heat until smooth. Remove from heat and stir in sugar, eggs, and vanilla. Add flour, baking powder, and salt; mix well. Stir in chopped walnuts.

Divide batter in half and spread each portion in a greased pan. Bake at 350⁰ until top is almost firm to the touch in the center, 30 to 35 minutes. Cool in pan on rack for 5 minutes. Run a knife around pan edge and turn out of pan onto cooling rack. Remove paper immediately. Cool.

Doris Oitzman   *Victor Valley High School*
Victorville

Chocolate Chip Valentine Cookie

Makes 2 Big Cookies

½ cup margarine
¾ cup brown sugar, packed
1 teaspoon vanilla
1 egg
1 cup plus 2 tablespoons all-purpose
    flour

½ teaspoon baking soda
½ teaspoon salt
1 6-oz. package semi-sweet chocolate
    chips
½ cup walnuts, chopped

Grease 2 heart shaped cake pans or 8" or 9" pans. Line bottoms with waxed paper, then grease paper.

In a large bowl, beat together margarine and brown sugar until creamy. Beat in vanilla and egg. Mix in the all-purpose flour and ½ teaspoon *each* baking soda and salt. Stir in semi-sweet chocolate chips and chopped nuts.

Divide dough in half and spread each portion in a greased pan. Bake at 375⁰ until lightly browned all over and center is almost firm to touch, about 15 minutes. Cool in pan on cooling rack 5 minutes. Run a knife around pan edge and turn onto rack. Remove paper immediatley. Cool.

For Gift Giving

You might seal the cookie in plastic. Line a baking sheet with paper towels and place it in a 325⁰ oven. Wrap each *cooled* cookie with heavy plastic wrap, taping at back. Place wrapped cookies slightly apart on the warm pan; leave in oven until plastic shrinks slightly, about 2 minutes.

"This recipe is fun to make, fun to give, and good to eat! It looks as good as a heart shape or as an over-sized chocolate chip cookie."

Doris Oitzman   *Victor Valley High School*
Victorville

St. Patrick's Day

Karstaedt's Irish Creme

Makes a scant quart

2 eggs
1 can eagle Brand condensed milk
1¼ tablespoon Hershey's chocolate
    syrup

½ pint cream or half and half
1 cup Irish whiskey
3 tablespoons white creme de menthe
½ teaspoon honey

Put all ingredients into a blender. Blend on high for one minute. Keeps in refrigerator for 5 months. Very similar to Bailey's Irish Creme.

"Good as an after dinner 'cap-off'".

Betsy Cosart

Monache High School
Porterville

Spinach Dip

Serves 6 to 8

1 8-oz. box chopped spinach
1 cup sour cream
1 cup mayonnaise

4 green onions, chopped
1 package Knorrs leak soup mix

Thaw spinach, squeeze to drain. Add sour cream, mayonnaise, onions and soup mix. Combine all ingredients. Let chill for 1 to 2 hours. Serve with chips, crackers, bread sticks, vegetables, etc.

"I hollow out a loaf of round bread and use as a serving dish. It's green and it's good!"

Marsha R. Martin

Auburndale Junior High School
Corona

Paddy's Split Pea Soup

Serves 30

4 cups dried split peas
1 large onion, chopped
3 quarts water
1 tablespoon salt

1 or 2 hambones
Juice, jelly and scraps of ham
1 quart milk
¼ teaspoon pepper

Put all ingredients except milk and pepper together in a 5 or 6 quart crockpot. Cook on low for 6 hours (or even more). Remove bone and skin from ham. Put remaining soup through the blender until smooth. Return to the crockpot; add milk and pepper. Cook on low for another hour.

"I've built a soup reputation with this family recipe. For standard cooking, cook 3 hours before adding milk and pepper . . . then another 2 hours."

Harriet Trousdale

T. Roosevelt Junior High School
Glendale

Mary's Mom's Irish Soda Bread

Serves 10 to 12

4 cups flour
4 teaspoons baking powder
½ teaspoon salt
1 cup sugar

1/3 cup butter
1 cup raisins
2 cups milk

Mix together in a large bowl, flour, baking powder, salt and sugar. Cut in butter with pastry blender. Stir in raisins. Add enough milk to make soft dough. Spoon into greased 12" cast iron skillet. Bake at 350⁰ for 1 hour.

Serve sliced hot or cold with butter.

"Boston Irish recipe handed down from generation to generation."

Susie Pendleton   ***Cerritos High School***
Cerritos

Frosted Jello Salad

Serves 10 to 12

1 large lime Jello
1 cup boiling water
2 cups gingerale
2 bananas, sliced

1 large can crushed pineapple
(drain and save juice)
1 cup miniature marshmallows

Dissolve Jello in boiling water. Cool until it reaches room temperature. Add remaining ingredients and let set (Do not use ice for quick-set method or the gingerale won't mix in.) When Jello is set, spread topping on it.

Topping
1 cup sugar
2 tablespoons flour
1 egg

1 cup pineapple juice
2 cups whipped cream or Cool Whip
½ cup grated cheddar cheese, optional

Combine sugar, flour and egg in saucepan. Slowly add juice, stirring constantly. Cook until thick (like pudding). Cool at room temperature and then refrigerate. Remove from refrigerator, fold in whipped topping. Sprinkle with grated cheese if desired for extra color.

"This salad is my children's first choice for Christmas and birthday celebrations."

Kathleen DeBelius   ***Mountain View High School***
El Monte

Stuffed Peppers

Serves 4

4 medium/large bell peppers,
    well shaped
1 pound ground beef or sweet
    sausage, browned
2 15-oz. cans Spanish rice
1 small can olives, chopped
4 large mushrooms, chopped

1 small zucchini squash, coarsly
    chopped
slivered almonds
4 oz. Monterey Jack cheese grated
2 tablespoons sweet basil
2 tablespoons parsley, chopped
1 large stalk crisp celery, chopped

Wash and core peppers; set aside. Brown beef. Rinse off excess fat with hot water and drain well. Chop mushrooms and zucchini. Grate cheese; set aside. Mix together meat, Spanish rice, olives, mushrooms, squash and almonds (reserve some almonds for garnish).

Stuff peppers. Place in a baking dish or individual baking dishes. Bake at 375° for 20 to 25 minutes or until peppers are just tender. Sprinkle well with cheese (let cheese melt a little). Garnish with remaining almonds. Serve as a main dish or at a buffet dinner.

"Easy to stuff ahead of time, cover and refrigerate until ready for baking. If served at a buffet, use small bell peppers and you'll have more servings."

Judi Topp   *Raney Junior High School*
                                                                    Corona

Surprise Spring Pie

Serves 4 to 6

1 *package frozen chopped spinach*	½ *teaspoon salt*
¼ *cup chopped green onion*	¼ *teaspoon pepper*
1 *cup shredded Swiss cheese*	2 *tablespoons melted butter*
2 *cups milk*	4 *eggs*
1 *cup Bisquick Mix*	

Thaw spinach. Combine spinach, onions and cheese. Place in the bottom of a well-buttered 10″ pie pan. Beat remaining ingredients by hand for one minute. Pour mixture over spinach mixture. Bake at 400° for 35 to 40 minutes. Allow to set for 5 minutes before serving.

"Our 8 year old daughter prepares this, and our entire family really enjoys it. It is so easy and so good!"

Angie Garrett   *Tenaya Middle School*
                                                                    Fresno

Corned Beef and Cabbage

Serves 8 to 10

3 *pounds corned beef*	4 *potatoes*
2 *cups water*	1 *onion, large*
1 *cabbage*	8 *carrots, small*

Place corned beef on a rack inside a pressure cooker. Add 2 cups water. Cook 60 minutes with pressure regulator rocking. When the pressure drops, drain the liquid and set the meat aside. To the liquid, add cabbage (in quarters), potatoes, chopped onion and carrots. Cook for 5 minutes under pressure. Cool and add the meat.

"This is a favorite recipe of my grandmother Marquerite Dolan."

Bonnie Landin   *Garden Grove High School*
                                                                    Garden Grove

Chocolate Mint Cake

Serves 20

1 box white cake mix
6 tablespoons green Creme de Menthe, divided

1 can Hershey's Chocolate Topping (yellow label)
1 8-oz. carton non-dairy topping

Mix cake according to package directions. Stir in 3 tablespoons of Creme de Menthe. Pour into a 9" x 13" greased and floured pan. Bake according to package directions. Cool cake completely. Spread with chocolate topping.

Topping
Mix the remaining 3 tablespoons of Creme de Menthe with the non-dairy topping. Spread over top of cake and refrigerate until ready to serve.

"A delicately flavored, pale green mint cake with chocolate filling."

Helen W. Williams   **North High School, Bakersfield**

Saint Patrick's Day Cookies

Makes 6 to 8 dozen

1 cup powdered sugar
1 cup granulated sugar
1 cup oil
½ pound butter, softened
2 eggs
1 teaspoon baking soda

1 teaspoon salt
1 teaspoon cream of tartar
1 teaspoon vanilla
4½ to 5 cups flour
2 teaspoons green food coloring

Cream together all of the above ingredients until smooth. Add 4½ to 5 cups of flour gradually to the creamed mixture. Divide dough into 2 bowls and add 2 teaspoons green food coloring to one bowl and mix in with a metal spoon. Add enough flour to make a dough which can be rolled in your hands without sticking to the palms. Roll dough into balls the size of a quarter or smaller. Then roll balls in graulated sugar or cake decorations added to sugar.

Put cookies on an ungreased cookie sheet. Flatten each dough ball with the bottom of a glass, which has been greased and sugared. Bake at 350⁰ for 12 to 15 minutes. Cookies should not turn brown, but remain white. Cool and serve.

"Cookies can be all white, all green or a combination of both. Be creative."

Marion Vickers   **Bartlett Junior High School, Porterville**

Pistachio Dessert

Serves 8 to 10

30 Ritz crackers
½ cup margarine
1½ cups milk
2 packages pistachio instant pudding

1 quart softened vanilla ice cream
2 envelopes dream whip (mixed according to package directions)
3 large Heath bars, crushed

Crush crackers and mix with melted margarine and press into a 9" x 13" pan. In a bowl, mix pudding and milk together according to package directions. Add softened ice cream, mix well. Pour over crumbs and spread whipped topping over pudding. Sprinkle with crushed Heath bars. Refrigerate until serving time.

Julie Chivers   **Tulare Union High School**
Tulare

"Green Stuff" Dessert

Serves 18

½ cup margarine
1 cup flour
½ cup nuts, chopped
1 cup powdered sugar
1 8-oz. package cream cheese
½ 8-oz. Cool Whip

3 cups cold milk
1 6-oz. package instant vanilla
  pudding
1 3-oz. package instant pistachio
  pudding

Combine the first 3 ingredients and press into a 9" x 12" pan. Bake at 350° for 20 to 25 minutes. Remove and set aside.

Cream sugar and cheese and fold in Cool Whip. Spread over cooled crust. Blend together milk and instant puddings. Pour over cheese layer. Cover with remaining half of Cool Whip and sprinkle with nuts.

Loretta Salau

Foothill High School
Bakersfield

Killarney Chocolate Pie

Serves 8

1 baked 9" pastry shell or
  crumb crust
1 cup semi-sweet chocolate Mini Chips
1 envelope unflavored gelatine
¼ cup sugar
2 eggs, separated
1½ cups milk

1 teaspoon vanilla
1 tablespoon creme de menth or
½ teaspoon mint extract
½ cup heavy cream
¼ cup sugar
3 or 4 drops green food color

Prepare pie crust; set aside. Place Mini Chips in medium mixing bowl; set aside. Combine gelatine and ¼ cup sugar in saucepan; add slightly beaten egg yolks and milk. Let stand 5 minutes to soften gelatine. Place over medium heat, stirring constantly, until gelatine dissolves and mixture thickens slightly. Do not boil. Remove from heat; add vanilla and pour 1 cup mixture over Mini Chips. Stir or whisk until melted. Add creme de menthe to remaining mixture in saucepan. Chill both mixtures, stirring occasionally, until they mound slightly when dropped from a spoon.

Beat heavy cream until stiff peaks form; fold ½ cream into chocolate mixture. Beat egg whites with ¼ cup sugar until stiff peaks form. Fold ½ into chocolate mixture; pour into pie shell. Chill.

Fold remaining whipped cream and stiffly beaten egg whites into mint mixture; add food color. Chill 10 minutes or until mixture begins to set; spoon onto chocolate layer. Chill. Before serving, garnish with chocolate shavings or curls.

Hershey Foods Corp. (Photo page 71)

Hershey, PA

Shamrock Chocolate Cookies

Makes about 3 dozen

½ cup butter or margarine
¾ cup sugar
1 egg
1 teaspoon vanilla
1½ cups unsifted all-purpose flour
1/3 cup unsweetened cocoa

½ teaspoon baking powder
½ teaspoon baking soda
¼ teaspoon salt
Shamrock Glaze (recipe below)
Satiny Chocolate Glaze (recipe below)

Cream butter or margarine, sugar, egg and vanilla in large mixer bowl until light and fluffy. Combine flour, cocoa, baking powder, baking soda and salt; add to creamed mixture, blending well. Chill about 1 hour or until firm enough to roll. Roll a small portion of dough at a time on lightly floured board or between 2 pieces of wax paper to ¼″ thickness. Cut with shamrock-shaped cutter; place on ungreased cookie sheet. Bake at 325⁰ for 5 to 7 minutes or until no indentation remains when lightly touched. Cool cookes on sheet 1 minute; remove to wire rack to cool thoroughly. Frost with Shamrock Glaze or Satiny Chocolate Glaze.

Shamrock Glaze

2 tablespoons butter or margarine
2 cups confectioners' sugar
1 teaspoon vanilla

2 to 3 tablespoons milk
Green food color

Melt butter or margarine over low heat. Remove from heat; blend in sugar and vanilla. Add milk gradually; beat until proper consistency. Blend in 2 or 3 drops green food color. About 1 cup glaze.

Satiny Chocolate Glaze

2 tablespoons butter
3 tablespoons unsweetened cocoa
2 tablespoons water

1 cup confectioners' sugar
½ teaspoon vanilla

Melt butter in small saucepan over low heat; add cocoa and water, stirring constantly until mixture thickens. Do not boil. Remove from heat; beat in confectioners' sugar and vanilla until smooth. Add additional water, ½ teaspoon at a time, until desired consistency. Makes about ¾ cup glaze. (Photo page 71)

Hershey Foods Corporation   *Hershey, PA*

Irish Hot Chocolate

Serves 6

3 tablespoons unsweetened cocoa
¼ cup, plus 2 tablespoons sugar
dash salt
¼ cup hot water

3 cups milk
6 tablespoons Irish Whiskey, optional
½ cup heavy cream, whipped

Combine cocoa, sugar and salt in medium saucepan; blend in water. Blend to boil over medium heat, stirring constantly; boil and stir 2 minutes. Add milk; stir and heat to serving temperature. Do not boil. Remove from heat. Pour 1 tablespoon whiskey in each 6-oz. cup or goblet, if desired. Add hot cocoa; stir. Top with whipped cream. (Photo page 71)

Hershey Foods Corporation   *Hershey, PA*

Easter

Easter Egg Candy

Makes 2 pounds

2 1-pound boxes powdered sugar
2 cups nuts, chopped
1 stick margarine
1 can sweetened condensed milk

1 small can flake coconut
½ block paraffin
1 12-oz. bag chocolate chips

Mix all ingredients except chocolate and paraffin and form into egg shapes. Chill. Melt chocolate chips and paraffin in top of double boiler. Using tongs, dip candy eggs in mixture. Place on waxed paper. Decorate with canned frosting if desired.

"Makes a nice gift to give to neighbors at Easter!"

Alcyone Bass   *Hamilton Junior High School*
                                          Long Beach

Chocolate Covered Easter Eggs

Makes 12 eggs

½ cup butter or margarine
1 6-oz. package chocolate pudding
    and pie filling (not instant)
½ cup milk
1 1-pound box confectioner's sugar,
    sifted
1 teaspoon vanilla

1 cup walnuts, chopped
5 squares unsweetened chocolate,
    melted and cooled or ¾ cup
    chocolate chips, melted
20 mini-marshmallows
assorted colored sugar

Melt butter in a 3 quart heavy saucepan. Stir in *pudding mix and blend until smooth. Gradually stir in milk. Cook over medium heat, stirring constantly, until mixture is very thick and starts to boil. Cook until mixture leaves the sides of the pan. Remove from heat.

Stir in confectioner's sugar and vanilla. Mix until smooth. Stir in walnuts. Cool until mixture is stiff enough to hold its shape.

Shape mixture into 12 eggs, using about 2 tablespoons mixture for each egg. Place on waxed paper lined baking sheet. Refrigerate 30 minutes. Dip each egg in cooled chocolate and place on cooling rack over waxed paper. If you wish to decorate with marshmallow flowers, place on egg before chocolate sets.

Flowers
Cut miniature marshmallows in thirds crosswise. Dip cut side of each piece in colored sugar. Arrange 5 pieces, sugared side up, on each egg to resemble flowers. Let stand until chocolate sets.

You may also decorate with pastel flowers using your favorite decorating frosting. Store in refrigerator.

Vanilla, coconut, and butterscotch pudding also make excellent fillings as long as they are not instant puddings.

Myrna Orr   *McFadden Junior High School*
                                          Santa Ana

Molded Marshmallow Eggs

Makes 24 eggs

Molds

Fill 2 large pans, 9" x 12" or larger, with flour so that it's an inch deep. Make egg-shaped depressions by pressing a clean plastic egg as deep as possible in the flour. Holes should be about ½" apart. **Note:** *Do not double recipe.*

6 tablespoons cold water
2 envelopes unflavored gelatin
½ cup water
1½ cups sugar

1 teaspoon vanilla
dash salt
other flavorings, optional
food coloring, optional

Soften gelatin in the 6 tablespoons cold water. Bring the ½ cup water, sugar and salt to a boil. Add gelatin and stir until dissolved. Let cool until just *barely warm.* In a narrow deep bowl, beat with an electric mixer for about 5 minutes. Mixture will look like whipped cream. Do not overbeat. Add vanilla and tint with food coloring if you like. Sometimes I also add ½ teaspoon strawberry flavoring to a recipe and tint the mixture light pink . . . delicious and pretty!

Heap each "mold" with marshmallow mixture. Let set in the refrigerator. Remove eggs after they have set up and dust off flour. Make sure both sides have flour on them and then dust off excess, that way they won't stick to each other. Flour can be saved for baking.

Dipping

Dip in chocolate or "white chocolate." Put chocolate in small deep oven-proof bowl. Preheat oven to 350⁰. **Turn oven off.** Put chocolate in the oven for 10 to 12 minutes or until soft. It will retain its shape while melting until stirred. Spear eggs with a fork and dip them quickly into chocolate and put them on a wax paper lined pan. You can tint white chocolate with pastel colors for variety. You can also decorate the eggs with designs or names.

"Easy enough to do with children and lots of fun!"

Glenell Fuller

Glendora High School
Glendora

Easter Nests

Serves 12 to 14

1 small can Eagle Brand
    condensed milk
8 tablespoons sifted cocoa
1 large bag shredded coconut

Easter candy, jelly beans
M & M's

In a saucepan, mix cocoa with milk, then stir in coconut until there is no milk left in the bottom. Mound by teaspoonsful on greased cookie sheets. With forefinger, push center to form "dish" in nests. Fill with 3 small candies and bake at 350⁰ for 15 minutes.

Francine Miller

Upland Junior High School
Upland

Marshmallow Chicks and Bunnies

Serves 18

½ cup cold water
2 envelopes unflavored gelatin
½ cup sugar
1 cup light corn syrup

1½ teaspoons vanilla
powdered sugar
Decorators' Frosting, recipe follows

Line the bottom of a 12" x 9" x 2" (across the top) baking pan with wax paper. Lightly grease paper.

Pour the water into a 2-quart saucepan. Sprinkle the gelatin over the water and let stand to soften — about 5 minutes. Stir constantly over low heat until the gelatin dissolves — about 3 minutes. Add the sugar and corn syrup; stirring constantly, cook until the sugar is dissolved — about 1 minute. Off heat, stir in the vanilla.

In the large bowl of an electric mixer, at high speed, beat the gelatin mixture until it thickens and is a soft marshmallow consistency — about 5 minutes. Turn into the prepared pan. With a lightly buttered spatula, spread evenly. Let stand, uncovered, at room temperature to dry for 8 to 12 hours.

Heavily dust a cutting board with powdered sugar. Turn out marshmallow mixture onto it. Carefully peel off wax paper. Dust top of mixture heavily with powdered sugar.

Grease 2" metal bunny and chick cookie cutters — do not use plastic cutters. Leaving ¼" between each, cut out shapes. Dust top and sides of shapes with powdered sugar.

Fit a pastry bag with a plain decorating tip (No. 3). Fill the bag one-half full with Decorators' Frosting. Pipe along top outer edges, outlining chicks with yellow and bunnies with pink frosting. Use blue for eyes. Let dry at least 5 minutes. Wrap separately in wax paper or plastic wrap and store in a tightly covered container.

Decorators' Frosting

1½ cups powdered sugar
1 large egg white

⅛ teaspoon cream of tartar

In the small bowl of the electric mixer stir together powdered sugar, egg white and cream of tartar. At high speed, beat for 8 minutes. Keep frosting covered with a damp paper towel. Place about 1/3 of the Frosting in each of 3 small bowls. Stir in several drops of food color until blended — yellow in one bowl, blue in another bowl and pink in the remaining bowl. There may be some leftover frosting which you can use to decorate sugar cookies cut in Easter shapes or on vanilla wafers.

"These are fun. You really can make marshmallows!"

Polly Frank

Lakewood High School
Lakewood

Chocolate Baskets

Serves a group

1 pound semi-sweet chocolate, chopped
Do NOT use chocolate-FLAVORED)

Place souffle dish or custard cup on small board or baking sheet, upside down. Press aluminum foil over the top and sides, letting it extend about 2" on the bottom. Press foil tightly around the bottom edge, making a sharp, definite edge. Smooth out the wrinkles in the foil.

In the top of a double (1" water in bottom) boiler, over low heat, slowly melt chocolate. Stir until smooth. Let sit off the heat about 15 minutes or until thick enough to pipe through a pastry bag. If it becomes too firm while working, remelt slightly.

Fit a pastry bag with #2 or #3 tip (writing tip). Fill with some of the chocolate. Pipe a continuous drizzle of chocolate in a lacy design over the bottom and side of the mold. Don't be concerned if the chocolate drips.

OR instead of using a pastry bag, drizzle the chocolate over the mold with a teaspoon.

Refrigerate or freeze 5 - 10 minutes until chocolate is firm. Repeat with a second layer in the same manner. Refrigerate or freeze until firm. Repeat with a third layer, refrigerate at least 20 minutes. Be sure the bottom is solid chocolate.

Remove souffle dish by carefully pulling it out from underneath the foil. Turn basket right side up and remove foil by slowly and carefully pulling it away from sides and bottom of basket. If using the pastry bag, pipe a decorative chocolate border around the top edge of the basket. Refrigerate while making the handle.

To make the handle, line a baking sheet that will fit into refrigerator or freezer with waxed paper. Measure the diameter of the basket; mark that width on waxed paper. Draw the shape of the handle with chocolate. Remove writing tip from coupler or use another pastry bag) and replace with a star tip. Using room temperature chocolate (it can't be too warm or the design won't show), pipe zigzag lines around the handle shape. Refrigerate. Attach to the basket with more chocolate.

This will keep in the refrigerator for ages. It can be filled with long-stemmed strawberries or tiny candy Easter eggs, or a scoop of ice cream.

Note: There should be heavy chocolate (over ¼") on the top of the mold (which will be the bottom of the basket) and about ¼" on the sides (but in dribbles so there are holes on the sides). Basket may be made without a handle.

Polly Frank

Lakewood High School
Lakewood

Noodle Nests

Serves 12 to 16

1 12-oz. package butterscotch
   pieces

4 cups chow mein noodles
small jelly beans

Cover cookie sheet with waxed paper. Melt the butterscotch pieces in a double boiler. Stir until smooth and creamy. Stir in the chow mein noodles until well coated. Drop the mixture by ¼ cupfuls, about 1" apart, onto the waxed paper. Make a hollow indentation in the center of each, using the back of a spoon. Fill each next with five jelly beans. Let stand until firm.

"You can make a nest full of eggs to decorate the top of a cupcake or round cake!"

Joanne Fial
                                               East Middle School
                                                         Downey

Party Divinity

Makes about 2¼ pounds

3 cups sugar
¾ cup light corn syrup
¾ cup water

¼ teaspoon salt
2 egg white
1¼ cups chopped nuts

In heavy 2 quart saucepan stir together sugar, corn syrup, water and salt. Stirring constantly, cook over medium heat until mixture comes to a boil. Without stirring, continue cooking until temperature on candy thermometer reaches 250° or until small amount of mixture dropped into very cold water forms a ball which is hard enough to hold its shape yet plastic. Just before temperature reaches 250°, in large bowl with mixer at high speed, beat egg whites until soft peaks form. Slowly pour in syrup, beating until soft peaks form and mixture begins to lose its gloss. Immediately stir in nuts. Drop by teaspoonsful onto waxed paper. Store in tightly covered container.

Karo Corn Syrup, Best Foods
Consumer Service Department
                                            Englewood Cliffs
                                                New Jersey

No-Cook Fondant

Makes 1-1/3 pounds

1/3 cup margarine
1/3 cup light corn syrup
1 teaspoon vanilla

½ teaspoon salt
1 package (1 lb.) confectioner's
   sugar, sifted
food color (optional)

In large bowl with mixer at medium speed beat margarine, corn syrup, vanilla and salt until smooth. Add confectioners sugar all at once. With wooden spoon, then with hands mix until smooth. Turn out onto board and knead until mixture is well blended and smooth. Tint and shape as desired. Store in cool place.

Flavored Patties
Follow recipe for No-Cook Fondant. Substitute any of the following for vanilla: 1 teaspoon peppermint or wintergreen flavoring, 2 teaspoons orange extract or 1 teaspoon lemon extract. Tint desired color with food color. Shape into balls and flatten or roll thin and cut into small rounds.

Recipe for "Party Divinity" on page 85 →
Recipe for "No-Cook Fondant" on page 85 →
Recipe for "Lollipops" on page 87 →
    85

Peanut Squares
Follow recipe for No-Cook Fondant. Mix in ¾ cup coarsely chopped unsalted peanuts. Roll out or pat to ½" thickness. Cut into squares.

Almond Diamonds
Follow recipe for No-Cook Fondant. Substitute 1 teaspoon almond extract for vanilla. Mix in ½ cup coarsely chopped, toasted, blanched almonds. Roll out or pat to ½" thicknes. Cut into diamonds.

Candied Fruit Squares
Follow recipe for No-Cook Fondant. Substitute rum or rum extract for vanilla, if desired. Mix in ½ cup finely chopped mixed candied fruit. Roll out to ½" thickness. Cut into squares.

Mocha Logs
Follow recipe for No-Cook Fondant. Add 2 teaspoons instant coffee powder. Shape into rolls, about 2" long and ½" thick. Roll in chocolate sprinkles.

Circus Balls
Follow recipe for No-Cook Fondant. Shape into ½" balls. Roll in multi-colored decors.

Nut Creams
Follow recipe for No-Cook Fondant. Shape into ½" balls. Press between 2 walnut or pecan halves.

Stuffed Dates
Follow recipe for No-Cook Fondant. Shape into very small finger-shaped rolls and stuff into pitted dates. Roll in graulated sugar. Makes enough to stuff about 1¾ pounds dates.

Chocolate Patties
Follow recipe for No-Cook Fondant. Add ¼ cup cocoa to sugar before sifting. Shape fondant into balls or roll thin and cut into desired shapes.

Easter Eggs
Follow recipe for No-Cook Fondant. Divide into 6 even pieces. Tint each a different pastel color. For pink, add 1 to 2 drops red food color. For peach, add 1 drop red and 1 drop yellow food coloring. For lavender, add 1 drop blue and 2 drops red food coloring. For yellow, add 2 drops yellow food coloring. For green, add 3 drops green food coloring. For blue, add 1 drop blue food coloring. Divide each colored batch in fourths. Form into egg shape. Place eggs on baking sheet and allow surface to dry a few hours. Decorate with decorators icing following manufacturer's instructions on labels. Add multi-color decors or silver and cold dragees, if desired. Makes 24 (2") eggs.

Ducks
Follow recipe for No-Cook Fondant. Tint 1 tablespoon bright orange. Tint remaining fondant yellow. for each duck, shape yellow fondant into ball. Elongate into an oval shape. Pull up end to form tail. For head, shape yellow fondant into small ball. Attach small piece or orange fondant for beak. Make eyes using wooden pick dipped in food color. Attach head to body.

Chocolate-Coated Almond Balls
Follow recipe for No-Cook Fondant. Shape into ½" balls. In top of double boiler melt 1 package (12 oz.) semi-sweet chocolate pieces. Stir in ½ cup Karo light corn syrup. Stirring constantly, cook 3 minutes. Remove from heat; keep over water. With fork dip fondant into chocolate and roll in 2 cups finely chopped unblanched almonds. If chocolate becomes too stiff for dipping, reheat. Refrigerate until set. Store in tightly covered container. Makes 7½ dozen. (2.2)

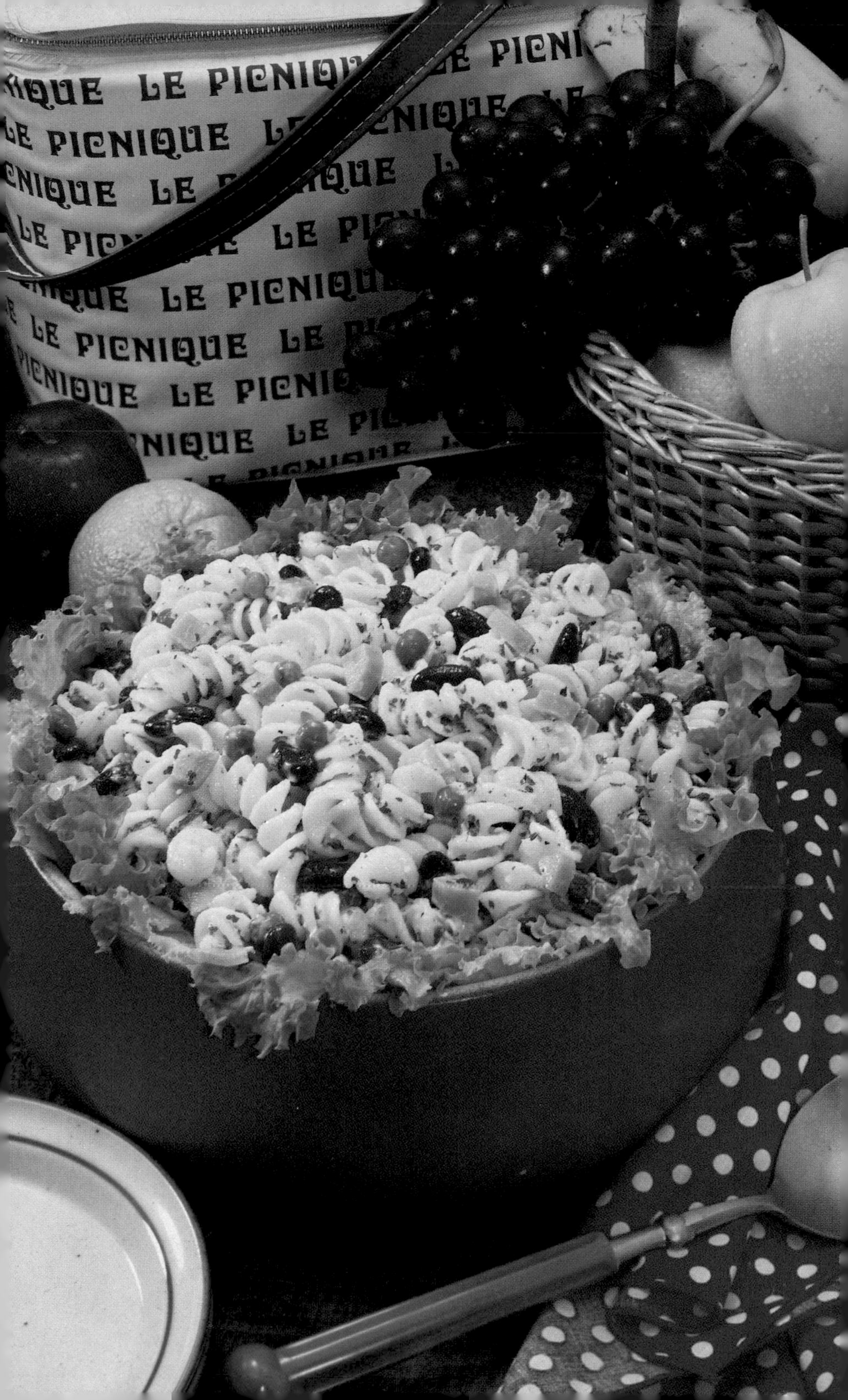

Lollipops
Makes 42

2 cups sugar
1 cup light corn syrup
½ cup water

1½ teaspoons peppermint, spearmint,
   lemon or orange extract
food color

In heavy 2-quart saucepan stir together sugar, corn syrup and water. Stirring constantly, cook over medium heat until mixture comes to boil. Without stirring, continue cooking until temperature on candy thermometer reaches 300° or until small amount of mixture dropped into very cold water separates into threads which are hard and brittle. Cool slightly. Stir in flavor and color just enough to mix. Place 42 lollipop sticks, 4" apart on greased baking sheets or foil. Drop candy mixture from tip of teaspoon over one each of each stick to form 2" disc. (If mixture hardens before all lollipops are made stir over low heat just until mixture is melted.)

Lollipop Faces
Prepare Decorator's Frosting. If desired, tint with food coloring. Pipe on lollipops to outline faces.

Lollipop Flags
Make molds as follows, using diamond shaped cutters and heavy duty or double thickness regular aluminum foil. For each, cut piece of foil 1" wider than cutter, and 1" longer. Grease one side of foil very lightly with margarine, then set cutter in center of greased side. Turn up foil all around bottom of cutter to make neat diamond shape. Carefully remove foil and place on flat surface. Close to bottom of mold and just to one side of a corner, make hole in one side of mold with skewer. Insert lollipop stick (dowel stick cut into 6" or 7" lengths), keeping stick parallel to one side of diamond. Prepare Lollipop mixture, using ¼ teaspoon oil of cinnamon or 1½ teaspoons peppermint extract and red food coloring. Immediately pour into molds to ¼" thickness, holding stick in place with one hand. Remove foil when candy is hard. If desired, pipe 6 stripes of Decorator's Frosting and field of blue Decorator's Frosting on each. Makes 18 flags using 3½" diamond shaped cutter, measured from top to bottom.

Note: If preferred, make 9 lollipop flags and pour remaining mixture into lightly greased 9" x 5" loaf pan. Continue as directed for Hard Candy Squares.

Lollipop Flowers
Prepare lollipop mixture; cool slightly. To make 3 different colors and flavors, divide candy mixture into 3 different small, hot, dry saucepans. Stir color and flavor into each using desired color and ¼ teaspoon desired flavoring. Drop candy mixture from tip of teaspoon over one end of each stick to form 2" disc. (If mixture hardens before all lollipops are made, stir over low heat just until mixture is melted.) Make as many lollipops as desired, up to 36, and drop remaining candy mixture by teaspoonsful onto greased baking sheet or foil. Prepare Decorator's Frosting. If desired, tint with food color. Pipe on lollipops. If desired, decorate with assorted cut-outs of No-Cook Fondant (recipe #924-d) attached with small amount of Decorator's Frosting.

Hard Candy Drops
Prepare Lollipop mixture; cool slightly. Add extract and color, stirring just enough to mix. Or for a variety of colors and flavors, divide candy mixture into 3 different small, hot, dry saucepans. Separately, color and flavor using desired color and ¼ teaspoon flavoring. Drop candy mixture by teaspoonsful onto cookie sheet or foil. (If mixture hardens, stir over low heat just until melted.) Makes about 75 pieces.

Hard Candy Squares

Prepare Lollipop mixture; immediately pour into greased 8" x 8" x 2" pan. Cool until film forms on top. Beginning at edge use a sharp knife to mark the candy into ½" squares. (Do not break through film.) Using flat metal spatula continue pressing along marks, pressing deeper each time. When spatula may be pressed to bottom of pan, candy will be shaped in puffs. Cool completely, turn out on board and break into pieces. Makes 256 pieces.

Microwave Directions

In 2-quart ovenproof glass bowl, stir together 1 cup sugar, ½ cup light corn syrup and 2 tablespoons water. Microwave with full power 2 to 3 minutes or until mixture boils and sugar is dissolved. Stir thoroughly. Microwave 4 minutes. Check temperature with candy thermometer. (*Do not use candy thermometer in microwave during cooking.*) Temperature should reach 300° or a small amount of mixture when dropped into very cold water should separate into threads which are hard and brittle. If temperature is below 300° microwave 1 to 2 minutes longer checking temperature after each minute. Stir in 1 teaspoon extract and food color. Continue as in basic recipe for Lollipops.

Decorator's Frosting

In small bowl of electric mixer, stir together 1½ cups unsifted confectioners' sugar, 1 egg white and ⅛ teaspoon cream of tartar. With mixer at high speed, beat 8 minutes. Keep remaining frosting covered with damp paper towel. Makes about 1 cup. (Photo page 85)

Kayro Corn Syrup, Best Foods　　　　　　　　　　　　*Englewood Cliffs*
Consumer Service Department　　　　　　　　　　　　　　*New Jersey*

Cream Cheese Fruit Dip

Serves a group

1 8-oz. package cream cheese　　　　　dash vanilla
1 cup powdered sugar　　　　　　　　1 oz. Grand Marnier
sour cream (see below)

Beat first four ingredients until creamy, adding sour cream, 1 tablespoon at a time, to obtain desired consistency. Add Grand Marnier. Refrigerate. Remove from refrigerator ½ hour before serving. Great with strawberries!

Variation *Substitute brown sugar and rum for sugar and Grand Marnier. Serve with fresh pineapple chunks.*

Marianne Atkins　　　　　　　　*Faye Ross Junior High School, Artesia*

Cottage Cheese/Strawberry Salad

Serves 4 to 6

1 16-oz. carton small curd
　cottage cheese
1 3-oz. package strawberry gelatin
1 9-oz. Cool Whip
½ to 1 basket strawberries
2 to 3 sliced bananas

Mix together cottage cheese and dry gelatin. Add Cool Whip, strawberries and bananas. Serve

"Do not make a day ahead, as fruit will not keep. It makes a nice cool, light salad."

Super Special Easter Eggs

Makes 6 eggs

6 large empty eggshells
2 envelopes unflavored gelatin
1 3-oz. package flavored gelatin
1½ cups boiling water

Grass
2 envelopes unflavored gelatin
1 3-oz. package lime gelatin
3 cups boiling water

To prepare eggshells, make opening at wide end of the egg, break yolk and allow contents to empty. Carefully rinse and air dry. Store in a clean egg carton. Refrigerate.

Dissolve gelatin in water. Cool 10 minutes. Using cup with pour spout, carefully fill each eggshell. Set in carton and chill until firm — about 5 hours.

To peel egg, remove shell, then membrane. If difficult to peel, *quickly* dip chilled egg into bowl of warm water, then peel.

Bed of Grass
Dissolve gelatin in water. Chill. When firm, take a fork and break surface to appear like grass. Set eggs on grass. You may garnish with a whipped cream border.

Cathy Bergeron   *Stanford Junior High School, Long Beach*

Frozen Orange Souffle Grand Marnier

Serves 4

3 egg yolks
¼ cup plus 2 tablespoons sugar
1 cup whipping cream

1½ oz. Grand Marnier
½ cup whipping cream, for garnish
4 orange shells

Cut top ¼ off each orange, hollow out with a spoon. In medium bowl, beat together egg yolks and sugar until stiff. Whip the 1 cup cream; fold into the yolk mixture; fold in the Grand Marnier. Spoon the mixture into the orange shells and freeze two hours or more. Whip the ½ cup cream, spoon over the top of the oranges just before serving.

George Yackey   *Santana High School, Santee*

Spinach Balls

Serves 4 6o 6

1 10-oz. package frozen, chopped
   spinach, cooked and drained
2 teaspoons onions, grated
2 teaspoons Swiss cheese, grated
1 egg
⅛ teaspoon allspice

1½ cups bread crumbs
salt and pepper to taste
1 egg
2 tablespoons water
1/3 cup vegetable oil

Combine spinach, onion, cheese, 1 egg, allspice, ½ cup bread crumbs, salt and pepper. Allow to stand 4 to 6 minutes for bread crumbs to swell. Form into 1" balls. Mix egg and water. Roll balls in remaining crumbs, in egg mixture and again in crumbs. Fry in oil for 3 minutes. Drain on paper towels and serve immediately.

Gift Idea Smnall basket with a ribbon tied to the handle. Place spinach balls inside.

"Serve on a platter garnished with carrot curls and parsley."

Dorothy J. Reynolds   *Hoover School, Merced*

Oatmeal Cutlets

Serves 4

4 eggs, well-beaten
1 large onion, sauted in oil
½ cup quick oats
1 cup walnuts, chopped

1 beef bouillon cube or imitation
   beef flavoring (George Washington
   makes a good one)
Ritz Crackers, finely crushed

Melt bouillon cube in ¼ cup hot wter. Mix all ingredients except the Ritz Crackers. Add enough crushed crackers to make mixture very stiff. (Depends on the liquid, but usually takes 20 to 30 crackers.)

Fry in hot oil until golden brown. Place in a baking dish and cover with sauce.

Sauce

1 can cream of mushroom soup
1 cup sour cream
1 cup grated cheese, cheddar
   or Jack

1 cup mushrooms, sliced
1 thinly sliced onion

Mix all of the above ingredients in a medium saucepan. Heat over medium heat, stirring frequently until cheese melts. Pour over oatmeal cutlets. Serve over rice.

"Terrific and tasty for your vegetarian friends or just a delicious switch from meat!"

Linda Hinson   *Diegueno Junior High School*
                                                                    Encinitas

Chestnut Puff

Serves 6 to 8

1 medium carrot, coarsely
   shredded
2 medium onions, chopped
2 tablespoons butter
½ teaspoon salt

1 15-oz. can chestnut puree
3 tablespoons port wine
4 egg yolks
2 oz. sliced almonds
4 egg whites

Preheat oven to 350⁰. Saute carrot and onions in butter. Place carrots and onion mixture in bowl and add salt, chestnut puree, port and egg yolks. Beat until well blended. Stir in ½ of the almonds. Beat egg whites until stiff. Fold into puree mixture. Pour into well-buttered souffle dish or shallow baking dish. Sprinkle top with remaining almonds. Bake at 350⁰ for 40 minutes or until puffed and brown.

"Try this instead of potatoes or yams with poultry or ham."

Susie Pendleton   *Cerritos High School*
                                                                    Cerritos

Special Sole

Serves 4

4 large sole fillets
dash of salt
dash of pepper
dash of garlic salt
2 tablespoons margarine
¼ cup minced onion

¼ cup minced mushrooms
¼ cup flour
¼ cup milk
¼ cup sharp cheddar cheese, shredded
½ cup cooked crab meat, flaked (optional)
½ cup white wine

Rinse sole fillets and pat dry. Season on both sides with salt, pepper and garlic salt to taste.

Melt butter in saucepan. Saute onion and mushrooms until tender. Combine flour and milk in another saucepan. Stir in cheese and cook over low heat, stirring constantly until cheese melts. Add onion and mushrooms; cook and stir for an additional 3 to 4 minutes.

Sylvia Kassap   *Paramount High School*

Beer-Batter Fish

Serves 12 to 16

½ cup flour
½ cup cornstarch
1 teaspoon baking powder
1 teaspoon sugar

1 teaspoon salt
1 egg, separated
1 tablespoon oil
beer

Mix together flour and cornstarch. Add baking powder, sugar and salt. Mix. In a separate bowl, mix together egg yolk and oil. Add to flour mixture. Add enough beer to make a soft batter. Whip egg white stiff and fold into batter, first. Dip your fish and fry.

Marilyn Pereira   *Hanford High School*
                                                                      Hanford

Chicken Asparagus Casserole

Serves 4

2 whole chicken brests
1½ teaspoons Accent
½ cup oil
20 ounces asparagus, fresh or frozen
1 can cream of chicken soup

1 cup sour cream
1 teaspoon lemon juice
½ teaspoon curry powder
1 cup sharp cheddar cheese, shredded

Cut chicken into 2″ x 2″ pieces, sprinkle with Accent. Saute chicken in oil about 6 minutes or until opaque. Remove and drain on paper towels, set aside.

Cook asparagus 4 to 5 minutes in a small amount of water. Drain. Place asparagus on the bottom of a 9″ x 9″ x 2″ baking dish and arrange chicken on top of asparagus.

In a bowl, blend together chicken soup, sour cream, lemon juice and curry. Pour mixture over chicken, spread evenly. Sprinkle on cheese and bake t 375⁰ for 30 minutes. Serve over rice.

Peggy   Stevens   *Santa Ynez Valley High School*
                                                                 Santa Ynez

Judy T's Chicken with Broccoli

Serves 4 to 6

1 cups cooked chicken, sliced
2 boxes frozen broccoli, cooked
   until half done
½ cup mayonnaise or sour cream
1 teaspoon lemon juice

½ teaspoon curry powder
2 cans cream of chicken soup
½ cup cheddar cheese, grated
   (optional)
Ritz Crackers (optional)

Grease casserole dish. Layer chicken and broccoli. Repeat. Mix mayonnaise (or sour cream), lemon juice and curry powder with soup. Cover chicken and broccoli with soup mixture. May be topped with grated cheese and crushed crackers. Bake at 350⁰ for 25 minutes.

Kathleen Daudistel

Hanford High School
Hanford

Crumb-Topped Baked Ham

Serves 10

1 fully cooked 10 to 12 pound ham
1/3 cup Dijon-sytle mustard
½ cup firmly packed light brown sugar
½ cup sherry
1¾ cup fresh bread crumbs
2/3 cup finely ground pecans
¼ cup snipped parsley

Sherried Mustard Sauce
2 tablespoons butter
2 tablespoons flour
1½ cups beef broth
2 bay leaves
6 tablespoons sherry
¾ cup sherry
6 tablespoons Dijon mustard

Place ham on rack. Trim off rind, then trim fat to ¼" thick. Bake at 325⁰ for 1½ hours. Score in 1" strips. Brush with mustard and sprinkle with brown sugar. Return to oven for 1 hour.

Topping
Combine sherry, bread crumbs, pecans and parsley; mix well. Gently pat crumb mixture onto alternate strips of scored ham. Continue to bake for ½ hour. Serve with mustard sauce.

Sherried Mustard Sauce
Melt butter in a saucepan. Stir in flour. Cook over medium heat stirring constantly for 1 minute. Gradually stir in beef broth, bay leaves and 6 tablespoons sherry while continuing to cook over medium, heat. Cook until thick and smooth; lower heat and simmer 5 minutes. Heat ¾ cup sherry in a saucepan until reduced to half. Stir in 6 tablespoons Dijon mustard. Gradually stir into broth mixture. Cook 5 minutes. Remove bay leaves. Serve over ham.

"An 'extra-special' Easter Ham!"

Gloria Reece

Porterville High School
Porterville

Orange Biscuits

Makes 12

2 cups flour, sifted
4 teaspoons baking powder
2 teaspoons sugar
½ teaspoon salt

1 tablespoon orange peel,
  grated
5 tablespoons butter
¾ cup fresh orange juice

Preheat oven to 425⁰.

Sift together flour, baking powder, sugar and salt. Cut in orange peel and butter, until mixture resembles coarse meal. Add orange juice. Mix to form a ball and knead 10 times. Roll to ½" thickness. Cut with floured cutter and bake at 425 degrees for 10 to 12 minutes.

Mrs. Sally Oxford   *Monache High School*
                                                              Porterville

Orange Popovers

Serves 8

1 cup sifted all-purpose flour
1 tablespoon finely grated orange
  zest
¼ teaspoon salt
1 tablespoon sugar

1 tablespoon vegetable oil
½ cup orange juice
½ cup milk
2 eggs

Preheat oven to 450⁰. Thoroughly butter eight 2½" muffin cups.

In a large mixing bowl, combine the flour, orange zest, salt and sugar. In a medium bowl, beat oil, orange juice, milk and eggs together until combined. Pour mixture into dry ingredients, beating with wire whisk until the batter is very smooth, for 2 to 3 minutes.

Pour the batter into the prepared cups, filling each about halfway. Bake for 30 minutes or until the popovers are deep golden brown. Serve at once.

Nan Paul   *Grant School*
                                                         Escondido

Easter Basket Muffins

Makes 10 muffins

¼ cup instant non-fat dry milk
1½ teaspoons baking powder
¼ teaspoon salt
¼ teaspoon allspice
¼ teaspoon nutmeg
½ teaspoon cinnamon
1½ cups whole wheat flour

½ cup honey
½ cup oil
2 eggs
½ teaspoon vanilla
½ cup grated apple
½ cup grated carrot
½ cup peanut M & M's

Combine dry ingredients. Combine moist ingredients. Mix the two together. Fold in grated apple and carrot. Pour into paper muffin liners in muffin tins and bake 15 minutes at 375⁰.

Immediatley after removing muffins from the oven, place peanut M & M's into the tops of the muffins as if arranging eggs in an Easter basket.

Kathryn Phillips   *Lincoln Middle School, Vista*

Streusel-Filled Coffee Cake

Serves 4 to 6

1½ cups sifted flour
3 teaspoons baking powder
¼ teaspoon salt
¾ cup sugar
1/3 cup shortening
1 egg
½ cup milk

Filling
½ cup brown sugar
2 teaspoons cinnamon
2 tablespoons flour
2 tablespoons melted butter
½ cup nuts, chopped

Sift flour, baking powder, salt and sugar together. Cut in shortening. Mix egg and milk together. Make a well in the center of the dry ingredients. Add liquid mixture and stir until all dry ingredients are moistened. Spread half of this mixture into a greased and floured 7" x 11" pan. Sprinkle with half of the streusel mixture. Add other half of the batter and sprinkle remaining streusel mixture over the top. Bake at 375⁰ for 25 to 30 minutes.

"Super great coffeecake! Can be doubled in a 9" x 18" pan. Good with coffee or milk anytime of the day."

Mary Lou Sommer

*Monte Vista Junior High School
Camarillo*

Hot Cross Buns

Makes 20 large buns

6 to 7 cups flour*
2 envelopes dry yeast
½ cup sugar
1½ teaspoons salt
½ cup softened butter
    or margarine

1-1/3 cups hot water
4 eggs, room temperature
½ cup finely chopped citron (optional)
½ cup currants or raisins (optional)
1 egg yolk
1 tablespoon milk

(This recipe easily adapts to cuisinart mixing.)

Combine two cups flour, the undissolved yeast, sugar and salt in a large bowl.

Add softened butter. Add hot tap water. Beat with electric mixer at medium speed two minutes, scraping bowl occaisonally. Add eggs, one at a time, then add 1½ cups more flour. Beat on high speed two minutes. Add citron and raisins, if desired.

Gradually stir in enough remaining flour with a wooden spoon to make a *soft dough* that leaves the sides of the bowl. Turn onto floured board and knead 5-10 minutes or until dough is smooth and elastic. Cover and let rise 20 minutes in a warm place.

Punch down dough. Divide into four parts, then divide each part into five equal size pieces. Shape each piece into a ball with a smooth top. Place on a well-greased 12" x 15" baking pan about 1" apart. Cover loosely with transparent plastic film Refrigerate overnight or up to 24 hours.

When ready to bake, uncover, let stand in a warm place 20 minutes. Bake below center of oven at 350⁰ for 15 minutes.
Combine egg yolk and milk. Remove pan of rolls from oven, brush tops with egg/milk mixture. Return to oven immediately and continue baking 10 to 15 minutes or until golden brown. When cool, make traditional crosses on top with cake decorator tube.

94

Lemon Frosting

1 cup sifted powdered sugar
2 teaspoons lemon juice

1 teaspoon water

Combine and beat until smooth.

For best results, use Gold Medal Flour.

Bonnie Pius

Sanger High School, Sanger

Brioche - Easter Rolls

Makes 36 rolls

1 cup milk
½ cup butter
1 teaspoon salt
½ cup sugar
2 packages dry yeast

4 eggs, beaten
1 teaspoon lemon peel
5 cups flour
melted butter

Scald milk, then stir in butter, salt and sugar. Cool to lukewarm. Sprinkle yeast on warm water and stir to dissolve. Combine eggs and lemon peel. Add to yeast; then add to milk mixture. Beat in flour, a little at a time, to make soft dough you can handle.

Turn onto floured board; knead lightly until dough is smooth and satiny. Place in greased bowl; turn dough over to grease top. Cover and let rise in a warm place free from drafts until doubled (about 2 hours). Punch down and turn onto floured board. Knead lightly.

Shape 2/3 of the dough into smooth 2" balls. Shape remaining dough into 1" balls. Place large balls in greased muffin pan cups. Flatten balls slightly, making a deep indentation in each with finger or handle of wooden spoon. Shape small balls (like teardrops) and set in each indentation. Brush with melted butter and let rise until doubled, about 1 hour. Bake at 425⁰ for about 10 minutes. Remove from pans at once.

"This recipe works great in the food processor using dough hook. Also, on Easter morning instead of the traditional hot cross buns, we love to have these!"

Beth Gurrero

Selma High School, Selma

Tsoureki - Easter Egg Bread

Serves 8 to 10

2 loaves frozen unbaked bread dough
½ cup mixed candied fruit
¼ cup blanched almonds

½ teaspoon anise seed
1½ teaspoons lemon peel, grated
5 raw eggs, colored

Defrost bread dough and knead the two loaves together. Mix together fruits, almonds, anise seed and lemon peel. Knead into bread dough.

Divide dough into three equal portions. Form each into a strand 28" long. Place strands parallel to each other and pinch the tops together. Braid the strands, then transfer braid to a greased cookie sheet, forming it into a ring. Pinch ends together.

Press colored eggs upright into the dough between braids. Cover and let dough rise until almost doubled, about 30 minutes. Bake according to frozen bread directions. Cool.

Re-tint eggs (if necessary) with a brush dipped in diluted food coloring. Frost with confectioner's sugar frosting. Sprinkle with colored sprinkles.

Frosting
1 cup confectioner's sugar	½ teaspoon vanilla
4 teaspoons hot milk	colored sprinkles

Mix first three ingredients together and frost bread, then add sprinkles.

Sharon Schooping Turner   **El Dorado High School**
                                               Placentia

Almond Pear Pie

Serves 8 to 10

1 baked pastry shell

Filling
Almond paste	4 egg yolks, slightly beaten
2/3 cup sugar	2 tablespoons butter
¼ cup cornstarch	½ teaspoon almond flavoring
½ teaspoon salt	2 teaspoons vanilla flavoring
3 cups milk	

Between two sheets of wax paper, roll out enough almond paste to cover bottom of pastry crust to ⅛" thickness.

In saucepan, combine sugar, cornstarch and salt. Blend milk and egg yolks, gradually stir into sugar mixture. Cook over medium heat, stirring constantly until mixture thickens. Boil and stir one minute. Remove from heat. Blend in butter and flavorings. Pour into bowl. Refrigerate until cold. Pour into baked pastry shell on top of almond paste.

Topping
5 to 6 canned pear halves, drained	1 cup whipping cream, whipped
1/3 cup apricot preserves, strained and heated	¼ cup sliced almonds.

Drain and pat dry pear halves. Arrange on top of cream filling with stem end toward center. Spoon apricot glaze over top of pears (use only enough to lightly glaze each pear). Garnish with whipped cream (use a pastry bag fitted with a star tip) and sprinkle with almonds.

Nancy Hunyadi   **Fullerton High School**
                                               Fullerton

Easter Nut Torte

Serves 16 (because it's so rich!)

12 eggs, separated
1 cup sugar
1½ teaspoon baking powder

¼ cup bread crumbs
3 cups walnuts, ground very fine
½ teaspoon vanilla

Beat egg yolks and sugar until light and fluffy. Mix together the baking powder and bread crumbs. Beat eggs whites until stiff. Take half the egg whites, half the nuts, half the bread crumbs and fold into the egg yolk batter *very gently*. Fold other half into batter with the vanilla. Divide batter evenly into three greased and floured 10" cake pans. Bake at 350⁰ for 25 to 30 minutes, or until toothpick comes out clean. Frost with icing below.

Chocolate Icing

9 eggs, separted
¾ cups sugar
1½ bars German Sweet Chocolate

¾ lb. cold sweet butter
1 teaspoon vanilla

Put yolks and sugar in top of double boiler and beat with mixer until light and fluffy. Cook over hot water for 10 to 15 minutes, stirring often. Break chocolate into small squares and add one square at a time to egg mixture, stirring constantly. Remove from double boiler. When cool, beat with mixer, adding butter slowly. Beat thoroughly, then add vanilla. Frost layers and top and sides of cake. Keep refrigerated at all times. Remove about 1 hour before serving.

"This recipe was given to my mother by an elderly lady from Yugoslavia in 1950, and has been a 'special occasion' dessert ever since!"

Janae Krol   ***Tustin High School, Tustin***

Lemon Spring Swirl Pie

Serves 6 to 8

Crust
1 cup all-purpose flour
½ teaspoon salt
1/3 cup shortening
1 egg, slightly beaten
1 teaspoon grated lemon rind
1 tablespoon lemon juice

Filling
¼ cup cornstarch
1/3 cup lemon juice
1 cup cold water
1 teaspoon grated lemon rind
2 egg yolks, slightly beaten
¾ cup sugar
4 oz. cream cheese
2 egg whites
¼ cup sugar

Sift flour and salt together. Cut in shortening. Mix egg, lemon rind and lemon juice. Sprinkle over flour mixture until moist enough to hold together. (If necessary, add a few drops of cold water.)

Roll out pastry on floured board to fit 9" pie pan. Put small leftover pieces of dough into another pan and bake (for crumbled topping on finished pie). Prick bottom and sides of pastry and bake at 400⁰ for 12 to 15 minutes. Let cool.

In a saucepan make a paste of cornstarch and lemon juice to avoid lumps. Add cold water, lemon rind, egg yolks and sugar. Cook over medium heat; stirring constantly until thick. Set aside to cool.

Mash cream cheese that has been kept at room temperature into large bowl with fork. Gradually add lemon filling a small amount at a time. Blend well and let mixture cool.

Meanwhile beat egg whites until soft mounds form. Gradually add ¼ cup sugar. Beat until stiff peaks form and fold into cooled lemon mixture. Spoon into baked pie shell.

Sprinkle top with crumbled pastry. Chill in refrigerator at least 2 hours before serving.

Cheryl Ann Oravetz   *Hemet High School*
Hemet

Yogurt Pie

Serves 6 to 8

1 large container of Cool Whip   1 graham cracker pie crust
2 containers of strawberry yogurt (16 oz.)

Allow non-dairy topping to defrost and mix thoroughly with yogurt. Slice fresh strawberries in bottom of pie crust. Add yogurt mixture and allow to set 5 minutes. Add strawberries on top. Refrigerate. Serve.

"May be made with any flavor yogurt and fruit."

Janae Krol   *Tustin High School*
Tustin

Heavenly Strawberry Cream

Serves 8 to 10

1½ cups sliced strawberries   2 cups whipping cream, whipped
¾ cup sugar   1 cup flaked coconut
¼ teaspoon salt   1 8-oz. can crushed pineapple, drained
¼ teaspoon almond extract   1 cup softened vanilla ice cream

Beat strawberries with sugar, salt and almond extract with mixer at high speed until fluffy. Stir in ice cream, coconut and pineapple. Chill while whipping cream. Fold strawberry mixture into whipped cream. Freeze until firm. Soften slightly before serving.

Mary Lash   *Paramount High School*
Paramount

Cinco de Mayo

Cheesy Bean Dip

Serves 12 to 15

1 can Dennison's Chili beans
  in chili gravy
1 8-oz. package cream cheese
1 cup sour cream

1 4-oz. can Ortega chiles, diced
2 packages Kraft sharp cheddar
  cheese, shredded
2 teaspoons instant minced onions

Place all ingredients in a blender, placing beans and chiles in first. Mix until
thoroughly blended, then heat in a double boiler, or in a saucepan over low heat
until cheese is melted. May be served hot or cold with corn chips or French
bread.

"This also makes a great filling for burritos, or topping for tostadas!"

Carole Delap   **Golden West High School**
                                                        Visalia

Hot Bean Dip

Serves a group

2 large cans refried beans
2 8-oz. packages sharp cheddar
  cheese
2 4-oz. cans green chili
  salsa

2 4-oz. cans diced chili
2 pounds bacon, cut into 1"
  pieces and fried
1 package pepperoni
6 large tomatoes

In a large saucepan, place all ingredients and mix well. Add tomatoes and a little
bacon grease. Pour all into a baking pan and bake at 450° for 1 hour. Serve with
corn tortilla chips.

Gage Jones   **South Pasadena High School**
                                                South Pasadena

Seven Layer Mexican Dip

Serves a group

1 16-oz. can refried beans
1 cup sour cream
1 cup guacamole
½ cup olives, chopped

1 8-oz. can died chilies
2 whole tomatoes, diced
1 cup sharp cheddar cheese,
  grated

On a serving dish, layer refried beans, then sour cream. Make up your favorite
recipe of guacamole and spread on top of the sour cream. Spread chopped olives
on top and refrigerate overnight.

Next day, layer or diced chilies, diced tomatoes and top with grated cheese. Serve
with your favorite chips.

Beverly Merrill   **Wangenheim Junior High School**
                                                        San Diego

Ortega Cheese Omelette Appetizer

Serves about 10

1 pound Velveeta cheese
1 8-oz. package cream cheese

1 large can Ortega chilies, chopped
crackers of your choice

Soften the Velveeta cheese and cream cheese, separately. Roll the Velveeta cheese into a round shape, about 10", like a pizza, between two pieces of wax paper. Roll it to about ¼" thickness. Spread ½ the softened cream cheese over the Velveeta in the shape of a half moon. Sprinkle the chopped chilies over the cream cheese. Fold the plain side over the cream cheese side. It will look like an omelette. Place a knife with it and crackers. People can cut through it and spread it on crackers.

"Goes great anywhere, at anytime. Can be prepared ahead of time, but seal it with plastic wrap, so it doesn't dry out. Refrigerate."

Penny Putnam   *Divisadero Junior High School*
Visalia

Taco Quiche

Serves 8

8 corn tortillas
2 pounds ground beef
1 onion, chopped
1 clove garlic, pressed
1 teaspoon chili powder
¼ teaspoon ground cumin
¼ teaspoon thyme
¼ teaspoon salt
½ teaspoon oregano

1 pound Jack cheese, shredded
6 eggs
2 cups milk
1 cup sour cream
2 tomatoes, sliced
1 avocado, sliced
1 small head lettuce, shredded
olives
salsa, optional

Line a greased 9" x 13" baking dish with tortillas, tearing to fit if necessary.

In a large skillet brown ground beef and onion. Add garlic, chili powder, cumin, thyme, salt and oregano. Pour into baking dish. Top with cheese. In a separate bowl, beat eggs with milk and pour over all. Bake at 350° for 1 hour, until custard sets. While still warm, spread with sour cream, then tomatoes, avocado, lettuce and olives. Pass salsa at the table, if desired.

"This is a meal in a single dish. very colorful!"

Marianne Estes   *La Mirada High School*
La Mirada

Walking Taco

Serves 8

2 tomatoes, seeded and diced
2 cans Frito bean dip
3 avocados, mashed
1 teaspoon lemon juice
2 heaping tablespoons sour
   cream

2 heaping tablespoons mayonnaise
½ package Lawry's Taco Seasoning Mix
4 oz. Jack cheese, grated
4 oz. cheddar cheese, grated
1 bunch green onions, chopped finely
1 small can black olives, chopped

Mash avocados and add lemon juice (you may substitute 2 cans frozen spicy guacamole). Mix together sour cream, mayonnaise and Lawry's Taco Seasoning and set aside.

Layer in a casserole dish: bean dip, avocados, sour cream mixture, grated cheeses, onion, tomatoes and black olives. Serve with chips.

Carol Lovett   *Horace Ensign School, Newport Beach*

Spanish Rice
Serves 8

1 cup uncooked rice	1 teaspoon salt
4 tablespoons oil	1 tablespoon chili powder
1 bell pepper, chopped	(dissolved in ¼ cup water)
1 onion, chopped	1 cup fresh tomatoes, chopped
1 small clove garlic, minced	1¼ cups water

Brown rice in oil. Add the garlic, bell pepper and onion. Saute lightly. Add salt and chili powder to the ¼ cup water, stir until well blended. Add to rice mixture. Cook on low heat for one minute, then add 1¼ cups water and chopped tomatoes. Cover and cook on low heat for 20 minutes. (*Do not stir while cooking.*) After 20 minutes, remove lid. Allow rice to set about 2 to 3 minutes, then fluff with a fork.

Linda Hinson   *Diegueno Junior High School*
                                                  Encinitas

Chile Relleno Casserole
Serves 6

1 7-oz. can whole green chilies	1 7-oz. can diced green chilies
1 pound Jack cheese, shredded	6 large or 8 medium eggs
1 pound sharp cheddar cheese, shredded	1 13-oz. can evaporated milk

Split whole chilies lengthwise. Remove seeds and membranes. Lay flat in bottom of a 9″ x 13″ pan. Mix cheeses. Top chilies with a layer of cheese. Alternate with the diced chilies. Repeat layers until chilies and cheese are used. Beat together the eggs and evaporated milk. Pour over cheese/chile mixture. Bake at 350⁰ 30 to 35 minutes.

Marguerite S. Darnall   *Corona Senior High School, Corona*

Mexican Delight
Serves 8

1 pound ground beef	2 cloves garlic, crushed
1 small onion, chopped	1 teaspoon Accent
1 can tomato sauce	1 teaspoon chili powder
1 can tomato paste	½ teaspoon whole cumin seed
3 paste cans of water	1 teaspoon salt
2 tablespoons sugar	1 cup cooked rice

Brown ground beef and onion. Add the rest of the ingredients, except the rice. Simmer 40 minutes covered. Add cooked rice. Serve with condiments over Fritos (regular size).

Condiments

avocados, in pieces
grated cheese
onion, chopped
salsa sauce

tomatoes, in pieces
lettuce, chopped
olives, sliced
sour cream

"Great for big crowds. Serve buffet style."

Brenda Umbro

San Marcos Junior High School
San Marcos

Sausage and Green Chile Strata

Serves 4 to 6

1 pound bulk pork sausage
5 slices white bread
soft butter or margarine
¾ pound (3 cups) shredded sharp
   cheddar cheese
4 eggs, slightly beaten

2 cups milk
½ teaspoon salt
½ teaspoon dry mustard
¼ cup green chilies, drained, rinsed,
   seeded and chopped

Crumble sausage in medium skillet; cook over high heat, stirring frequently until meat is browned. Drain off excess grease; set aside. Remove crusts from bread; lightly butter one side of each slice and cut into cubes. Place half the bread cubes in bottom of buttered 8″ square baking dish; sprinkle with half the cheese and cover with the fried sausage. Place remaining bread cubes over sausage and top with remaining cheese.

Combine eggs, milk and seasonings; pour over cheese and bread cubes. Cover and refrigerate several hours or overnight. Before baking, sprinkle with chopped green chilies. Bake uncovered at 350⁰ for 1 hour or until golden brown and set.

"I like this for brunch because it can be made ahead of time."

Pam Ford

Temecula Valley High School
Temecula

Bunuelos (Mexican Puff Pastry)

Serves 8 to 12

3¼ cups flour
½ teaspoon salt
½ cup shortening
¼ cup sugar
1 egg, beaten

¾ cup warm water

Topping
1 cup sugar
1 tablespoon cinnamon

Sift together flour and salt; set aside. Cream shortening and sugar together until soft. Add beaten egg and beat well. Alternately add flour mixture and warm water. Make into small balls. Put a little shortening on hands and roll each ball between hands. Let sit about 1 hour. Roll flat with rolling pin. Fry in about 1″ hot oil. Brown each side. Sprinkle with cinnamon and sugar while hot.

Audrey Stock

Sequoia Freshman
Fresno

Mother's & Father's Day

Egg Sausage Souffle

Serves 6

4 to 5 slices sourdough bread, cubed
2½ to 3 cups cheddar cheese
1½ pounds link sausage
4 large eggs
¾ teaspoon dry mustard

2¼ cups milk
1 can cream of mushroom soup
¼ can milk
1/3 cup chives, chopped, or green
    onion tops

Take 5 large slices of sourdough bread and cut into cubes ½" to ¾". Place in a greased 9" x 13" pan. Grate cheddar cheese and sprinkle on bread. Brown sausage, drain, and cut into pieces ½" long. Place on top of cubed bread. Beat together eggs, dry mustard and 2¼ cups milk. Pour over all. Cover and refrigerate overnight.

Before baking, dilute cream of mushroom soup with ¼ cup milk. Pour over all. Sprinkle casserole with chopped chives. Bake, uncovered, at 325⁰ for 1 hour. Serve immediately

Leota Hill   *Saddleback High School, Santa Ana*

Breakfast Casserole

Serves 6 to 8

8 slices white bread
1½ pounds sausage, cut up
¾ pound sharp cheddar cheese
4 eggs, beaten

3 cups milk
¾ teaspoon prepared mustard
1 can mushroom soup
4-oz. can mushrooms

Remove crust from bread and cut into cubes. Fry sausage. Grate cheese. Mix together bread, sausage and cheese and place in a casserole dish. Mix egg, 2½ cups milk and mustard. Pour over ingredients in casserole and refrigerate overnight.

Before baking, add mushroom soup and ½ cup milk. Add 4-oz. can of mushrooms. Bake at 300⁰ for 1½ hours.

Jennifer Gierman   *Ball Junior High School, Anaheim*

Northwoods Cheese Spread

Serves a group

1 pound cheddar cheese
2 oz. Romano cheese
1½ pounds margarine
½ teaspoon (or more) garlic powder

½ teaspoon paprika
few drops Tobasco sauce
2 teaspoons Worcestershire sauce
2 drops red food coloring

Grate cheese and combine with remaining ingredients. Mix with electric mixer until light, smooth and creamy — about 45 minutes. Yes, 45 minutes! If mixer motor heats up, let it cool down, then continue. (I've tried it for less time, and the results aren't as good.)

Spread thick layer on bread slice and place under broiler until mixture is bubbly and slightly browned.

"I package this in round margarine containers, then freeze until ready to use. Nice for a special dinner, after school snack, or those midnight munchies!"

Carol Goddard   *Alhambra High School, Alhambra*

Sweet and Sour Braised Onions

Serves 8

1 cup chicken stock
½ pound bacon, thickly sliced
    and cut into ¼" pieces
2 pints small white onions
1 tablespoon butter
1 tablespoon olive oil

3 tablespoons dark brown sugar
1 bay leaf
½ teaspoon dried thyme
salt and pepper to taste
3 tablespoons wine vinegar
1 tablespoon granulated sugar

Boil chicken stock until it has reduced to ½ cup; set aside. Blanch bacon in boiling water for 3 minutes. Drain on a double layer of paper towels.

Bring a 4 quart saucepan of water to a boil, drop in onions, and immediately remove pan from heat. Remove onions a few at a time and peel off the outer skin. Set onions aside.

Heat butter and oil over moderate heat. Add bacon pieces and saute, stirring often, until lightly browned. Transfer bacon to a dish and discard all but 3 tablespoons fat from skillet. Add onions to the skillet and shake pan over heat until browned on all sides. Add brown sugar and cook, shaking pan, for 2 minutes. Add the reduced stock, bay leaf and thyme and season with salt and pepper. Lower heat to simmering temperature.

In a small dish, stir togethr the vinegar and sugar and add the mixture to the skillet. Add the bacon bits. Partially cover pan and simmer 15 minutes or until the onions are tender Raise heat to high and cook until pan juices are syrupy —about 5 minutes.

"Serve hot or cold with a roast duck for a memorable Father's Day."

Gloria Reece   **Porterville High School**
                                                    Porterville

Dad's Barbecue Buns

Serves 8

1 small can ripe olive slices
1 12-oz. can corned beef
¼ cup mayonnaise

1 tablespoon prepared mustard
2 teaspoons instant minced onion
8 hot dog buns

Place corned beef in a bowl and shred with fork. Add olives, mustard, mayonnaise and onion. Stir.

Scoop out ¼" of hot dog buns and fill with mixture. Wrap in foil. Heat over hot coals or in very hot oven (450⁰) for 15 minutes.

"Quick and easy. Make in the morning and have ready for BBQ later. (Keep in refrigerator. Better make extra — they go fast!"

Joan Allan   **Los Cerritos Intermediate School**
                                            Thousand Oaks

Flank Steak

Serves 3 to 4

¾ cup oil
¼ cup honey
¼ cup teriyaki sauce
2 tablespoons vinegar

2 tablespoons green onion,
   finely chopped
1 large clove garlic, minced
1½ teaspoons ground ginger
flank steak

Mix all ingredients (except steak) together. Pour over steak and marinate overnight, turning occasionally. Barbeque about 10 minutes on each side over hot fire. Baste while cooking. Slice thin diagonally.

"Everyone loves this! I serve it with pilaf, spinach salad and an 'in season' fresh vegetable. It's an easy, delicious meal for a family gathering. I double it (or more) and marinate 3 to 4 steaks."

Kathleen Meadows   *Roosevelt Junior High School*
Selma

Dad's Favorite Barbecued Spare Ribs

Serves 6

1 large onion, chopped
½ cup celery, chopped
2 tablespoons bacon fat
1 tablespoons brown sugar
1 tablespoon Worcestershire sauce
2 tablespoons vinegar

½ teaspoon dry mustard
4 tablespoons lemon juice
1 small bottle of catsup
salt and pepper to taste
3 to 5 pounds country-style
   spare ribs

Brown country style ribs in an open 9" x 13" pan for about 1 hour at 350⁰.

While ribs are browning, in a medium saucepan, brown onion and celery in bacon fat. Add brown sugar, Worcestershire sauce, vinegar, dry mustard, lemon juice, catsup, salt and pepper. Cook over medium heat for 20 minutes. Pour sauce over ribs and bake one hour covered at 350⁰. Remove cover and bake 30 minutes longer.

"This was a prized family recipe of a neighbor who brought it from Arkansas about 50 years ago. I've never found anyone who didn't enjoy them served with a potato casserole and green salad."

Harriett Trousdale   *T. Roosevelt Junior High School*
Glendale

Heavenly Hamburger

Serves 6

1 pound ground beef
1 clove garlic, cut fine
1 teaspoon salt
dash of pepper
1 teaspoon sugar
2 8-oz. cans tomato sauce

1 8-oz. package noodles
6 green onions, cut fine (tops also)
1 3-oz. package cream cheese
1 cup sour cream
1 can water chestnuts, cut up
½ cup grated cheese

Scramble fry ground beef, drain. Add seasonings and tomato sauce to hamburger. Cook the noodles according to package directions. Drain.

Mix together onions, cream cheese, sour cream, water chestnuts and beef mixture. Toss gently into the noodles. Pour into baking dish and sprinkle with grated cheese. bake at 350° for 20 minutes.

"This recipe is similar to some of our Creative Casseroles that were prepared in class. Super for Mom's night off!"

Mary Lou Sommer

Monte Vista Junior High School
Camarillo

Chicken Cordon Bleu

Serves 6

6 chicken breasts, bone
6 thin slices boiled ham
6 1-oz. strips Swiss cheese
¼ cup flour
2 tablespoons butter
½ cup water
1 teaspoon chicken flavored
    gravy base

1 3-oz. can sliced mushrooms,
    drained
1/3 cup sauterne
2 tablespoons flour
½ cup cold water
toasted, sliced almonds to
    garnish

Pound chicken breasts. Place a piece of ham and cheese on each breast. Tuck in sides and roll together. Secure with toothpick. Coat with flour and brown in butter in a frypan. Remove to baking pan.

Add water, gravy base, mushrooms and sauterne to frypan. Heat, stirring in crusty bits. Pour over chicken. Cover and bake at 350° for 1¼ hours. Remove, and place chicken on a serving dish.

Blend flour with cold water. Add to liquid in pan. Pour a small amount of gravy over chicken. Serve remaining gravy on the side. Garnish with almonds.

"Perfect for an elegant meal!"

Nancy Horn

Selma High School, Selma

Chicken in Orange Sauce

Serves 4

½ teaspoon salt
2 chicken breasts, cut in half
2 tablespoons margarine
1 tablespoon flour
½ teaspoon salt
⅛ teaspoon cinnamon

dash of ginger
¾ cup orange juice
¼ cup white raisins
¼ cup slivered almonds
½ cup Mandarin orange sections

Sprinkle chicken lightly with salt and brown in margarine, remove from skillet. Add flour, salt and spices to skillet drippings, stir to make a paste. Gradually add orange juice and stir until thick. Stir in raisins and almonds.

Arrange chicken pieces in flat baking dish and pour sauce evenly over all pieces. Cover with foil and bake at 350° for 45 minutes. Garnish with Mandarin orange slices and serve with spiced rice pilaf.

"Very easy and inexpensive, but tastes and looks elegant!"

Susie Pendleton

Cerritos High School
Cerritos

Sweet and Sour Trout

Serves 8

6 tablespoons butter
¼ cup bell pepper, chopped
½ cup onion, chopped
1 8¼-oz. crushed pineapple
1 tablespoon sugar
1 tablespoon cornstarch

1 tablespoon vinegar
1 tablespoon pimento, chopped
4 trout, cleaned
1 egg, beaten
1 cup flavored bread crumbs
shredded coconut

Melt 2 tablespoons butter in a sauce pan. Add pepper and onion. Saute until soft, but not brown. Stir in undrained pineapple and sugar. Dissolve cornstarch in vinegar and add to mixture. Cook, stirring constantly, until mixture comes to a boil. Stir in pimentos — keep warm.

Dust trout with flour. Dip into egg and roll in bread crumbs. Fry in remaining 4 tablespoons of butter until brown on both sides and fish flakes easily with a fork. (About 5 minutes on each side.) Serve immediately with pineapple sauce and shredded coconut.

J.J. Wood   *Stephens Junior High School, Long Beach*

"Just for Mom" Bran Muffins

Serves 28 to 30

1 cup boiling water
3 cup bran buds
1½ cups granulated sugar
½ cup shortening
2 eggs

2 cups buttermilk
2½ teaspoons baking soda
2½ cups flour
1 teaspoon salt

Pour 1 cup boiling water over *1 cup* bran buds. Cool completely.

Cream sugar, shortening and eggs. Stir in buttermilk and bran/water mixture. Add baking soda, flour and salt. Add two remaining cups bran buds, stirring just until all dry ingredients are moistened. Bake at 400° in greased muffin pans for 15 to 20 minutes. The batter may be stored in an air-tight container in the refrigerator for 6 to 7 weeks! *Do not stir between bakings!*
"A very tasty muffin ready to bake without the hassle of making the batter each time."

Lois Armstrong   *Sonora High School, La Habra*

Applesauce Brownies

Serves 9

2 squares unsweetened chocolate
½ cup margarine or butter
1 cup sugar
2 eggs
2/3 cup applesauce

1 cup flour
¼ teaspoon salt
½ teaspoon baking powder
¼ teaspoon baking soda
½ cup walnuts, chopped

Melt chocolate and margarine together in a saucepan. Stir in sugar, eggs and applesauce. Add flour, salt, baking powder, soda and chopped walnuts. Mix. Bake at 350° for 25 to 30 minutes in a greased 8″ x 8″ pan.

Marilyn Pereira   *Hanford High School, Hanford*

Buttermilk Brownies

Serves a group

2 cups flour	2 eggs, beaten well
2 cups sugar	½ cup buttermilk
2 sticks butter	1 teaspoon baking soda
1 cup water	1 teaspoon vanilla
4 tablespoons cocoa	1 teaspoon cinnamon, optional

Sift flour and sugar, set aside. In a saucepan, boil together butter, water and cocoa. Pour over flour mixture and beat for 2 minutes. Add beaten eggs, buttermilk, baking soda and vanilla (cinnamon, if you wish). Beat 2 minutes and pour into greased 11" x 7" pan. Bake at 350⁰ for 20 minutes.

Frosting

1½ cups sugar	½ cup chocolate chips
6 tablespoons margarine	1 teaspoon vanilla
6 tablespoons milk	1 cup walnuts, chopped

In a saucepan, boil together sugar, butter and milk for 2 minutes. Add chocolate chips and beat until spreading consistency. Add vanilla and nuts. Frost brownies.

Dorothy Wilson   *Dale Junior High School*
Anaheim

Fresh Apple Cookies

Makes 3½ dozen

½ cup shortening	2 cups flour, sifted
1-1/3 cups brown sugar	1 teaspoon baking soda
½ teaspoon salt	1 cup unpared apples, finely
1 teaspoon cloves	chopped
1 teaspoon nutmeg	1 cup raisins
1 teaspoon cinnamon	1 cup nuts, chopped
1 egg, unbeaten	¼ cup apple juice

Combine shortening, brown sugar, salt, cloves, nutmeg, cinnamon, and egg; mix well. Sift flour with baking soda. Add half of flour mixture to shortening mixture and blend. Stir in apples, raisins, nuts and apple juice. Add remaining flour and mix well. Drop teaspoons of dough onto a greased baking sheet. Bake at 400⁰ for 11 to 14 minutes. Remove cookies from baking sheet and while still hot, spread with a thin coating of vanilla glaze (below).

Vanilla Glaze

1½ cups confectioner's sugar, sifted	¼ teaspoon vanilla
	⅛ teaspoon salt
1 tablespoon soft margarine	2½ tablespoons scalded milk

Combine all ingredients in a bowl and beat until creamy. Spread on cookies. Makes enough glaze for tops of 3½ dozen cookies

Gift Idea: *Use a see-through cookie jar, glass or plastic.*

Dorothy J. Reynolds   *Hoover School*
Merced

Mom's Lemon Meringue Pie

Serves 6 - 8

1½ cups sugar
3 tablespoons cornstarch
3 tablespoons all-purpose flour
dash salt
1½ cups hot water
3 egg yolks, slightly beaten

2 tablespoons butter or margarine
½ teaspoon grated lemon peel
1/3 cup lemon juice
1 9"-baked pastry shell,
    cooled

In a saucepan, mix sugar, cornstarch, flour and salt. Gradually add hot water, stirring constantly. Cool and stir over moderately high heat until mixture comes to boiling. Reduce heat, cook and stir two minutes longer. Remove from heat.

Stir a moderate amount of hot mixture into egg yolks, then return to hot mixture. Bring to boiling and cook two minutes, stirring constantly. Add butter and lemon peel. Slowly add lemon juice, mixing well. Pour into pastry shell. Spread meringue over filling and seal to edge. Bake at 350° for 12 to 15 minutes. Cool before cutting.

Note: *For creamier filling, cook and stir first five ingredients eight minutes over low heat after mixture comes to a boil. Blend in egg yolks as above, cook four minutes after mixture boils.*

Never Fail Meringue

2 tablespoons sugar
1 tablespoon cornstarch

½ cup cold water

Mix above ingredients together until cornstarch is dissolved. Then cook over medium heat stirring constantly until mixture is thick and clear. Cool.

3 egg whites
½ tablespoon vanilla

6 tablespoons sugar

Beat egg whites and vanilla until soft peak stage. Add sugar gradually, 1 tablespoon at a time, beating after each addition. Add cornstarch mixture and continue beating until meringue stands in stiff peaks. Pile on pie (while filling is warm) and cover to the crust making sure there are no holes. Bake at 350° for 12 to 15 minutes or until golden brown.

Paula Levand   **Canyon High School, Canyon Country**

Pineapple Walnut Dessert

Serves 10 to 12

7½ oz. package vanilla wafers,
    crushed
1 cup butter or margarine
1 cup extra fine granulated sugar
2 eggs
2 teaspoons vanilla
1 cup walnuts, finely chopped

2 cups crushed pineapple,
    well drained

Optional
8 oz. whipped cream
maraschino cherries
mandarin oranges

Crush vanilla wafers to fine crumbs (makes about 2 cups). Reserve 2 tablespoons. Cream butter to consistency of mayonnaise. Add sugar gradually, while continuing to cream. Add eggs one at a time, beating well after each addition. Add vanilla and mix well.

Combine pineapple and walnuts. Stir in until well mixed. Line a loaf pan, 3" x 5" x 8", with foil, leaving overhang so loaf can be lifted out easily. Press ½ cup crumbs on bottom of pan. Add about ¼ pineapple mixture, spreading evenly. Repeat until crumbs and pineapple mixture are used up, ending with pineapple mixture.

Scatter reserved crumbs on top. Chill 24 hours or longer (or you may freeze). Unmold and garnish with whipped cream, maraschino cherries or Mandarin oranges, if desired. Slice to serve.

"Can substitute powdered sugar for extra fine granulated sugar."

Sylvia Kassap   *Paramount High school*
                                                                Paramount

Chocoberry Torte

Serves 8 to 10

1½ cups unsifted all-purpose flour
1 cup sugar
¼ cup unsweetened cocoa
1 teaspoon baking soda
½ teaspoon salt
1 cup water
¼ cup plus 2 tablespoons vegetable oil

1 tablespoon vinegar
1 tablespoon vanilla
2 cups non-dairy whipped topping,thawed
    or 2 cups sweetened whipped cream
1 cup sliced sweetened strawberries,
    raspberries, or favorite fruit

Assemble ingredients; preheat oven to 350⁰. Grease and flour two 8" layer cake pans; set aside.

Measure flour, sugar, cocoa, baking soda and salt into mixing bowl; stir until combined. Add water, oil, vinegar and vanilla; beat with spoon or wire whisk until batter is smooth. Pour into prepared pans dividing evenly. Bake at 350⁰ for 22 to 25 minutes or until tester inserted in center comes out clean.

Remove from oven, place on wire racks to cool 5 minutes. Remove from pans; cool completely. Place one layer on serving plate; spoon 1 cup topping onto cake layer; top with second layer and remaining topping.

Before serving, arrange sliced sweetened strawberries or fruit, well drained, on top of torte. (If desired, increase fruit to 2 cups, arrange 1 cup between layers; remainder on top.) (Photo on cover)

Hershey Foods Corporation   *Hershey, PA*

Double Chocolate Delight

Serves 6 to 8

½ cup milk
1 8-oz. milk chocolate bar or
    two 4-oz. bars
½ cup semi-sweet chocolate Mini
    Chips
1 cup graham cracker crumbs
2 tablespoons sugar

3 tablespoons melted butter or
    margarine
1 cup heavy or whipping cream
sweetened whipped cream or topping
sliced sweetened strawberries or
    favorite fruit

Assemble ingredients. Place in saucepan; heat just to boiling point. Remove from heat; immediately add chocolate bar broken into pieces and Mini chips. Allow chocolate to melt, stirring occasionally until mixture is smooth. Pour into mixing bowl; cool to room temperature.

112

Meanwhile, combine graham cracker crumbs, sugar and melted butter; pat firmly into bottom of 8″ square pan. Chill.

Whip 1 cup cream until stiff peaks form; add to chocolate mixture folding gently just until blended. Pour onto chilled crust; freeze several hours or until firm.

To Serve: Cut into squares and top with dollop of sweetened whipped cream or topping; garnish with strawberries or favorite fruit. (Photo on Cover)

Hershey Foods Corporation   **Hershey, PA**

Dad's Favorite Chocolate Fudge Cake

Makes 1 tube cake

1 teaspoon baking soda
½ cup buttermilk
2 cups sugar
2 cups flour
1 teaspoon salt
1 cube margarine

1 cup water
½ cup oil   rounded tablespoons Hershey's
*   cocoa powder*
2 eggs, slightly beaten

Mix together baking soda and buttermilk. Set aside and allow to "bubble." In a large bowl add sugar, flour and salt. Set aside.

In a saucepan place margarine, water, oil and Hershey's cocoa powder; bring to a boil stirring constantly. Add four mixture; mix well. Add buttermilk mixture and beat. Add eggs and beat well. Pour into greased tube pan and bake at 350° for 45 minutes or until done.

Topping
1 cube margarine
¼ cup milk
3 rounded tablespoons cocoa

2½ to 2¾ cups sifted
*   powdered sugar*
1 teaspoon vanilla

Place all ingredients into a saucepan and bring to a boil stirring constantly. When it comes to a boil add the sifted powdered sugar and vanilla. Stir. Pour over the hot cake.

Dorothy Wilson   **Dale Junior High School**
Anaheim

Dad's Dessert

Serves 12

2 small packages instant vanilla
*   pudding*
3 cups milk
12 oz. carton non-dairy topping

3 bananas
1 box graham crackers
1 can milk chocolate frosting

Prepare the pudding using *three* cups of milk. Stir in the non-dairy topping.

Place a single layer of graham crackers in a 9″ x 13″ pan. Spread on 1/3 of the pudding mixture. Slice one banana onto the pudding. Repeat the layers ending with graham crackers. Chill. When it is firm, spread on the chocolate frosting. Chill 3 to 4 hours before serving.

Judy Thomas   **Washington Middle School**
La Habra

Mississippi Mud Pie

Serves 6 to 8

7½ oz. or 21 chocolate sandwich
    cookies
¼ cup sweet butter, melted
2 pints coffee ice cream
1 oz. (1 square) unsweetened chocolate

2 oz. (2 squares) semi-sweet chocolate
1 tablespoon plus 1½ teaspoons water
2 tablespoons light corn syrup
½ tablespoon sweet butter, cut
    into small bits

Crust

Line a 9" pie plate with a 12" square of foil. Press foil firmly into place by pressing against it with a pot holder. Fold the edges of the foil tightly out over the rim of the plate. Set aside. Break cookies into pieces and place in a food processor or blender, and process or blend until the crumbs are fine. (You should have a scant 1¾ cups of crumbs!) In a bowl, mix the crumbs thoroughly with ¼ cup melted butter. Turn the mixture into the lined pie plate. With your fingertips, distribute the crumbs evenly and loosely over the sides and then over the bottom. Then press the crumbs firmly against the sides — be careful that the top edge of the crust is not too thin — and press crumbs firmly against the bottom. It must all be very firm. No loose crumbs. Place in freezer at least several hours or overnight as it must be frozen firm

Filling

Place ice cream in refrigerator 10 minutes or so, depending on the firmness of the ice cream and the temperature of the refrigerator. Ice cream needs to be softened slightly so you can transfer it to the pie plate. Meanwhile, to remove foil from the pie plate, raise the edges of the foil and carefully lift it (with the frozen crust) from the plate. Gently peel away the foil (it should come away easily in 1 piece) by supporting the bottom of the crust with your left hand and peeling the foil slowly, a little at a time, with your right hand. As you peel, rotate the crust gently on your left hand. Support the bottom of the crust with a small pancake turner and ease it back into the plate very gently, so as not to crack it. It will not crack if it has been frozen sufficiently. Turn the slightly softened ice cream into the crust. Spread it smoothly, mounding it a bit higher in the middle. Return to the freezer until the ice cream is very firm.

Chocolate Glaze

Chop both kinds of chocolate into small pieces and set aside. Place the water, corn syrup and 1½ tablespoons butter in a small saucepan over moderate heat. Stir occasionally until mixture comes to a boil. Add chopped chocolate and remove from the heat immediatley. Stir with a small wire whisk until the chocolate is melted and the mixture is smooth. Set aside to cool to room temperature. Pour the cooled glaze carefully over the frozen ice cream to cover the top completely, being careful not to let any run over the sides of the crust. If it is necessary to spread the glaze, do it quickly before it hardens. It will be a very thin layer. Return the pie to the freezer at least a few hours or more. When the glaze is frozen firm, the pie may be wrapped airtight with clear plastic wrap and may be frozen for any reasonable time. This may be served with whipped cream (sweetened and flavored with vanilla or rum or bourbon) and toasted sliced almonds or other nuts.

Diane Everitt

Killingsworth Intermediate
Hawaiian Gardens

Pound Cake

Serves 16 to 20

2 cubes margarine
3 cups sugar
6 eggs
1 teaspoon vanilla

1½ teaspoons lemon extract
½ pint whipping cream
3 cups flour

Beat margarine with a beater until smooth. Add sugar and beat well. Add eggs and beat well. Add vanilla and lemon extract, then whipping cream and beat. Add flour and beat well. Pour into a greased tube or Bundt pan. Bake at 325⁰ for 1 hour and 40 minutes or until knife inserted in center comes out clean.

"Freezes well!"

Nancy Smith *Home Economist, Whittier*

Creamy Orange Sherbet

Serves 10

2¼ cups fresh orange juice
Juice of 1 lemon
2½ cups sugar

2½ cups heavy cream
1 quart milk

Mix together orange juice, lemon juice and sugar. Immediately before freezing, add heavy cream and milk. Freeze according to manufaturer's directions that accompany your ice cream freezer.

"Tastes like orange whipped cream!"

Carole Delap *Golden West High School, Visalia*

Father's Day Almond Torte

Makes 1 cake

1-2/3 cup whipping cream
3 eggs, beaten well
3 squares (3 oz.) unsweetened
    chocolate, melted and cooled
1 teaspoon almond extract
2½ cups all-purpose flour
1½ cups sugar
2¼ teaspoons baking powder

½ teaspoon salt

Frosting/Filling
2 cups whipping cream
1½ teaspoon almond extract
½ cup sifted confectioner's sugar
chocolate shot
almonds

Heat oven to 350⁰. Grease and flour two oblong layer pans, 8" or 9" x 12" x 1". Whip cream until stiff. Fold in eggs, chocolate and almond flavoring. Blend flour, sugar, baking powder and salt; fold gently into cream-egg mixture until well blended and batter is uniformly brown. Pour into pans. Bake 9" layers 30-35 minutes, 8" layers 35 to 40 minutes or until wooden pick inserted in center comes out clean. Cool. Split to make four layers, mark with wooden picks and cut with serrated knife.

Frosting/Filling
Beat whipping cream with almond extract, gradually adding confectioner's sugar until stiff. Fill layers and frost top of cake using ¼ (about ¾ cup) of the whipped cream for each layer. Form ring around top edge with chocolate shot. Decorate with almonds. Chill.

Lillian Lee *Hanford Joint Union High School, Hanford*

Americana

Lincoln Bell's Chocolate Cream Pie (Lincoln's Birthday)

Serves 6

¾ cup powdered sugar
½ cup butter
4 oz. bitter sweet chocolate
　(2 oz. German sweet chocolate
　plus 2 oz. Hershey's unsweetened
　chocolate)

½ teaspoon vanilla
3 eggs
1 cup cream, whipped

Cream the powdered sugar and butter, whipping generously. Melt chocolate over low heat or in the top of a double boiler. Cool and beat into the sugar and butter mixture. Add the vanilla and eggs, one at a time, beating thoroughly after each addition at high speed. Whip the cream and fold into the chocolate mixture. Pour into baked pastry and refrigerate at least 4 hours before serving.

Pie Crust — May be used for any pie

9 double or 18 single graham
　crackers, crushed
¼ cup sugar (up to 1/3 may
　be used)

¼ cup melted butter or margarine,
　softened (up to ½ cup may be used)

Combine crumbs and sugar. Add softened butter and mix well. Press into a 9" pan and chill about 45 minutes until set. Cool thoroughly before filling. If preferred, crust may be baked 10 minutes at 400° to brown. Cool and fill.

Lou Helen Yergat   **Mission Viejo High School**
Mission Viejo

Lincoln Logs

Makes three dozen

4 squares unsweetened chocolate
2/3 cup butter
4 eggs, beaten
2 cups sugar
1 cup flour
1 teaspoon baking powder
1 teaspoon salt
2 cups nuts, chopped

Frosting
1 teaspoon vanilla
2 squares unsweetened chocolate,
　melted
2 cups sifted powdered sugar
2 tablespoons cream or milk (add
　more if needed)
1 teaspoon vanilla

Melt chocolate and butter together in microwave. Beat eggs with electric beater, add sugar, and continue to beat until light in color. Add flour, baking powder, salt and nuts. Beat just until mixed. Add vanilla and mix. Spread batter into greased 9" x 13" pan. Bake at 350° for 40 minutes. Cool slightly then frost.

Frosting
Mix all ingredients together and beat with electric beater until smooth. (Frosting should be heavy enough to hold its shape.) Frost brownies. Make wavy vertical lines with a fork in the frosting to simulate texture of logs. Cut into rectangular shapes. Decorate a few with paper American flags if desired.

Martha Ford   **T. Roosevelt Junior High School**
Glendale

Nine Layer Dinner (Lincoln's Birthday)

Serves 10 to 12

8 oz. elbow macaroni or rotelle
6 to 8 oz. shredded Swiss cheese
½ to ¾ pound diced cooked ham
1 10-oz. package frozen peas
1 16-oz. can whole tomatoes, diced

1 12-oz. can whole kernel corn
2 oz. diced pimentos
1 10¾-oz. can cream of celery soup
½ cup milk or half and half
1 cup soft bread crumbs

Cook macaroni in salted water, drain. Place macaroni in greased 9″ x 13″ baking dish. Cover with Swiss cheese. Add layer of ham and peas. Place layers of tomatoes, corn and pimento. Thin soup with milk or half and half. Pour over pimento. Spread soft bread crumbs over casserole top. Bake at 350⁰ for 30 to 40 minutes.

Tips
When cooking macaroni for casserole, cook macaroni 3 to 5 minutes less than package instructions.

To conserve energy and prevent pasta from sticking together, stir pasta into boiling water to which you have added 1 tablespoon salad oil or margarine. Boil for 3 minutes, stir, cover and remove from heat. Allow to set until tender. Drain, rinse with cold water for salad, hot water if using in a casserole immediately.

Mary Lash   *Paramount High School, Paramount*

Delightful Cherry Squares (Washington's Birthday)

Serves a group

1½ cubes butter
2 cups all-purpose flour
1 cup nuts, chopped

2 1-lb. cans cherry pie filling
2 envelopes dream whip
1 8-oz. package cream cheese

Cut butter into flour; mix in nuts. Put in 7½″ x 12″ pan and bake at 400⁰ for 15 minutes. After cooling spread on cherry pie filling. Mix two envelopes of dream whip according to package directions. Add cream cheese to the dream whip. Spread on top of pie filling and refrigerate to chill.

"Gets better with time — will last a week."

Mary Hemmeter   *Los Alamitos High School, Los Alamitos*

Special Cherry Pie (Washington's Birthday)

Serves 6

1 3-oz. package cream cheese
½ cup powdered sugar
2 teaspoons vanilla

½ pint whipping cream
1 can cherry pie filling
9″ baked pie shell

Soften cream cheese; add powdered sugar a little at a time until well blended and add vanilla. Fold into beaten whipping cream. Place ¾ of the mixture in the bottom of a baked pie shell and put cherry mixture on top. Swirl remaining cream mixture around top edge of pie. Refrigerate several hours before serving.

Erma Jean Crider   *Sanger High School, Sanger*

118

Jambalaya (Mardi Gras)

Serves 12

¼ cup oil	5 cups stock or water with bouillon
1 chicken, cut up or bones	3 heaping teaspoons salt
1½ pound sausage	cayenne pepper
4 cups onions	1 cup green onions
2 cups celery	1 cup parsley, chopped
2 cups bell pepper	1 heaping tablespoon brown sugar, optional
1 tablespoon garlic, chopped	½ tablespoon Kitchen Bouquet, see below
4 cups long grain rice	½ tablespoon paprika, see below

Saute sausage in oil. Remove from pot. Season and brown chicken, remove from pot. For brown jambalaya, add heaping tablespoon brown sugar to oil and caramelize. For red jambalaya, delete this step.

Saute onions, celery, bell pepper, and garlic until vegetables are tender. Return chicken and sausage to pot, and simmer with vegetables. Add liquid and bring to boil. For brown jambalaya, instead of adding brown sugar, add ½ tablespoon Kitchen Bouquet. For red jambalaya, add paprika.

Add salt and pepper, then add rice and return to a boil. Cover and reduce heat to simmer. Cook for 30 to 35 minutes without peeking. (When cooking 6 or more cups of rice, it is necessary to move rice away from sides of pot 10 minutes after covering. Add green onions and parsley, and chopped tomatoes if desired. For seafood jambalaya, add seafood now.

Note: Liquid to rice ratio: 1 cup raw rice to 1¼ cups liquid; 1 cup raw rice feeds 3 people.

Kathie Baczynski   Mt. Carmel High School, San Diego

Bread Pudding (Mardi Gras)

Serves 16 to 20

1 10-oz. loaf stale French bread, crumbled or 6-8 cups any type bread	2 tablespoons vanilla
	1 cup raisins
4 cups milk	1 cup coconut
2 cups sugar	1 cup pecans, chopped
4 tablespoons butter, melted	1 teaspoon cinnamon
3 eggs	1 teaspoon nutmeg

Combine all ingredients; mixture should be very moist, but not soupy. Pour into buttered 9" x 9" baking dish. Place into non-preheated oven. Bake at 350° for approximately 1 hour 15 minutes, until top is golden brown. Serve warm with sauce.

Whiskey Sauce

½ cup butter	1 egg, yolk or whole
1½ cups powdered sugar	½ cup bourbon, to taste

Cream butter and sugar over medium heat until all butter is absorbed. Remove from heat and blend in egg yolk. Pour in bourbon gradually to your own taste, stirring constantly. Sauce will thicken as it cools.

For a variety of sauces, just substitute your favorite fruit juice or liquor to compliment your bread pudding. Bananas, peaches, pears, chocolate chips and amarreto can be substituted.

Kathie Baczynski   Mt. Carmel High School, San Diego

Spaghetti Carbonara-White Spaghetti (Ground Hog Day)

Serves 6

1 pound spaghetti
½ pound bacon, diced
1 large bell pepper, diced
3 eggs
½ teaspoon leaf marjoram, crumbled

½ teaspoon salt
dash pepper
½ stick butter
1 cup Romano cheese, grated
    (may substitute Parmesian)

Cook spaghetti as directed. Fry bacon until crisp, drain, reserving grease. Saute bell pepper in 2 tablespoons bacon fat. Beat eggs in a small bowl and add marjoram, salt and pepper. Toss butter with hot spaghetti until melted. Add seasoned eggs and toss until completely blended. Add bacon, peppers and grated cheese. Toss once more and serve at once.

"For our family of five I always double this recipe. It taste great cold, too. (If it lasts that long!)"

Angie Garrett   Tenaya Middle School, Fresno

Barbecued Chicken Drumettes (Memorial Day)

Serves 6 to 8

2 packages chicken drumettes
salt and pepper to taste
2/3 cup Kraft Hickory Smoked
    Barbeque Sauce

⅛ teaspoon garlic powder
⅛ teaspoon onion powder
1 teaspoon liquid smoke
1 tablespoon honey

Grease a large cookie sheet with shortening. Wash and pat dry chicken drumettes; then lay on cookie sheet closely, but not touching. Season to taste with salt and pepper. Cook in a 350⁰ oven for 40 minutes. Mix remaining ingredients to make the sauce.

Check chicken for doneness. Drumettes should be well done. Apply sauce to chicken and return to oven for 15 minutes. Turn each drumette and liberally apply remaining sauce. Raise temperature to 450⁰ and cook chicken for 5 to 7 minutes longer. Watch closely; the sauce is done when caramelized (and slightly burned) to the drumette. Remove from cookie sheet. Cool. Refrigerate for 3 to 4 hours before serving.

"Store in a flat container, not plastic bag as sauce will coat the bag and not your drumettes."

Virginia A. Green   Vista High School, Vista

Frozen Blackberry Yogurt (Memorial Day)

Makes 1 gallon

4 cups whole fresh blackberries (or
    unsweetened frozen, defrosted)
2 cups sugar
4 teaspoons lemon juice

4 teaspoons vanilla
3 eggs, beaten
2 quarts plain unflavored yogurt

Puree berries in blender or food processor. Combine with all other ingredients in a *very large* bowl. Mix well, using a wire whip if necessary to smooth out any lumps. Transfer to a gallon or larger size ice cream freezer. Freeze according to manufacturer's directions, using about 4 parts ice to 1 part rock salt. Other fresh or frozen fruit can be used in place of the blackberries.

"This is one of my husband's favorite recipes. It has about half the calories of homemade ice cream!"

Penny Niadna   *Golden West High School*
Visalia

Pasta Salad (Memorial Day)

Makes about 6 cups

1 cup real mayonnaise
½ cup chopped parsley
¼ cup grated Parmesian cheese
2 tablespoons lemon juice
1 clove garlic, minced or pressed
1 teaspoon dried basil leaves

1 package (8 oz.) macaroni
   (twists, shell or elbow), (2 cups),
   cooked, drained
1 can (16 oz.) red kidney beans, well drained
1 cup frozen peas, thawed, drained
1 cup coarsely chopped carrots

In a large bowl, stir together real mayonnaise, parsley, cheese, lemon juice, garlic and basil until smooth. Add macaroni, beans, peas and carrots; toss to coat well. Cover; refrigerate at least 2 hours to blend flavors. (Photo on page 86)

Hellman's Best Foods   *Englewood Cliffs*
Consumer Service Department   *New Jersey*

Frozen Chocolate Pecan Pie (Memorial Day)

Serves 6 to 8

Crust
2 cups pecans, toasted and
   finely chopped
5 tablespoons, plus 1 teaspoon,
   firmly packed brown sugar
5 tablespoons butter, chilled
   and cut into small pieces
2 teaspoons dark rum

Fillling
6 oz. semi-sweet chocolate
½ teaspoon instant coffee powder
4 eggs, room temperature
1 tablespoon dark rum
1 teaspoon vanilla
1½ cups whipping cream
2 tablespoons shaved semi-sweet chocolate

Crust
Blend first four ingredients together until mixture holds together. Press into bottom and sides of a 9″ pie plate. Freeze for at least 1 hour.

Filling
Melt chocolate with coffee in top of a double boiler over hot water. Remove from heat and whisk in eggs, rum and vanilla until mixture is smooth. Let cool about 5 minutes.

Whip 1 cup cream until stiff. Gently fold into chocolate mixture, blending completely. Pour into crust and freeze. About 1 hour before serving, transfer pie to refrigerator. Whip remaining ½ cup of cream and dollop or pipe over pie. Sprinkle with chocolate shavings.

"Pie can be frozen up to three months!"

Marilyn Pereira   *Hanford High School, Hanford*

Kona Inn Banana Bread
(King Kamehemeha Day, June 11)

Makes 2 1½-pound loves

1 cup butter or margarine	2½ cups flour, sifted
2 cups sugar	1 teaspoon salt
6 or 7 ripe bananas, mashed	2 teaspoons baking soda
4 eggs, well beaten	

Cream together margarine and sugar until light. Add bananas and eggs and mix well. Sift together flour, salt and baking soda. Blend dry ingredients into creamed mixture, being sure not to overmix. Pour batter equally into 2" x 4" x 8" loaf pans which have been lightly oiled and floured. Bake at 350⁰ for 45 to 50 minutes.

"This is an especially rich, moist bread, and keeps better than most, if you have any left over! Almost like a dessert."

Betsy Cosart   *Monache High School*
Porterville

Avocado Apple Salad (Fourth of July)

Serves 8

1 pound green eating apples, cored and sliced	4 tablespoons whipping cream
	salt to taste
3 tablespoons lemon juice	freshly ground black pepper
¾ cup mayonnaise	2 large ripe avocados

Sprinkle one of the sliced apples with 1 tablespoon of the lemon juice and reserve. In a bowl, mix the mayonnaise with the remaining lemon juice and the cream, salt and pepper

Halve the avocados and remove the stones. Peel off the skin, slice the flesh and fold through the mayonnaise immediatley. Fold in the apple slices and add more seasoning if needed. Cover and chill well before piling into a salad bowl for serving. Garnish with the reserved apple slices.

Note: *Polish the apples with a clean dry cloth before slicing. Serve with "Chilled Summer Soup."*

Nan Paul   *Grant School, Escondido*

Chilled Summer Soup

Serves 8

1 large bunch of watercress, trimmed	3 pints milk
	1½ pounds frozen peas
3 oz. butter or margarine	salt to taste
6 oz. onions, peeled and thinly sliced	freshly ground black pepper
	8 oz. whipping cream

Reserve a few watercress sprigs for the garnish and chop the remainder. Melt the butter in a saucepan and add the chopped watercress and onions and cover. Cook gently for about 15 minutes without browning. Take off the heat and stir in the milk, peas and seasoning. Then bring to a boil, stirring.

Cover and simmer gently for about 30 minutes or until the peas are really soft. Cool slightly, then puree in blender or food processor. Pour into a large bowl, add more seasoning if needed and cool. Stir in the cream and chill well before serving; garnish with the reserved watercress sprigs.

"Serve with your favorite French or sourdough bread and butter and Avocado Apple Salad!"

Nan Paul   *Grant School*
                                                     Escondido

Cauliflower Salad Bowl

Serves 8 to 10

4 cups raw cauliflower, thinly   ½ cup salad or olive oil
    sliced   3 tablespoons lemon juice
1 cup pitted black olives, sliced   3 tablespoons wine vinegar
2/3 cup bell pepper, coarsely   2 teaspoons salt
    chopped   ½ teaspoon sugar
½ cup pimento, chopped   ¼ teaspoon pepper
½ cup onions, chopped

In a medium bowl, combine cauliflower, olives, bell pepper, pimentos and onions. Set aside. In a small bowl, combine oil, lemon juice, vinegar, salt, sugar and pepper. Beat with rotary beater until well blended. Pour over cauliflower mixture. Refrigerate covered until well chilled — 4 hours or overnight. To serve, toss salad well and spoon salad into a bowl lined with lettuce leaves.

"A colorful and exciting tasting salad!"

Shirley Rusche   *Norte Vista High School*
                                                     Riverside

Grandma's Vegetable Salad

Serves 12 to 16

2 16-oz. cans cut green beans   1 bell pepper, sliced
1 16-oz. can sliced carrots   1 cup celery, sliced
1 red onion, sliced   1 teaspoon salt
½ cup sugar   1 teaspoon pepper
½ cup oil   ½ cup mayonnaise
½ cup vinegar   sweet pickle juice to taste
1 16-oz. can green peas

Drain green beans and carrots and combine with onion slices. Mix sugar, oil and vinegar, pour over vegetables and marinate overnight. Drain one hour. Add peas, bell pepper and celery. In separate bowl, combine salt, pepper, mayonnaise and sweet pickle juice to taste. Toss with vegetables. Chill at least one hour. Serve.

"We always include this in our Fourth of July BBQ menu. It never fails to get compliments. It's great!"

Penny Niadna   *Golden West High School*
                                                     Visalia

123

Fourth of July Layer Salad

Serves a group

1 package cherry gelatin
2 packages lemon gelatin
1 package raspberry gelatin
1 small can crushed pineapple

1 14½-oz. can blueberries
½ pint sour cream
2 cups milk
3 cups boiling water

Dissolve cherry gelatin in 1 cup boiling water. Cool. Add pineapple, mix and pour into the bottom of a gelatin mold.

Dissolve lemon gelatin in 1 cup boiling water. Cool. Beat together milk and sour cream and pour into lemon mixture. When cherry gelatin is firm and slightly sticky to the touch, gently pour lemon mixture over it.

Dissolve raspberry gelatin in 1 cup boiling water. Cool. Add blueberries and pour on top of lemon mixture, when lemon mixture is firm and slightly sticky to the touch.

Cleone Hatwan   *Paramount High School, Paramount*

Sonora Fruit Salad

Serves a group

1 11-oz. can mandarin orange
   segments
½ cup mayonnaise
½ cup dairy sour cream
2 bananas, sliced

1 8¼-oz. can pineapple
   chunks, drained
1 cup miniature marshmallows
½ cup shredded coconut

Drain orange segments, reserving 2 tablespoons syrup. Combine syrup, mayonnaise and sour cream; mix well. Add orange segments and remaining ingredients; mix lightly. Chill several hours or overnight.

Note: *Vary the fruit as you like, but be sure to select those that will keep overnight, such as apricots, peaches or cherries. Berries should be added just before serving. Like all salads, this creamy fruit mixture should be kept tightly covered in the refrigerator.*

Elizabeth A. Iorillo   *James Monroe Junior High School*
                                                    Ridgecrest

Spaghetti Salad

Serves 20 or a large group

1 pound spaghetti
2 teaspoons salt
½ teaspoon fine pepper
2 teaspoons coarse pepper
3 tablespoons Salad Supreme
½ cup Italian dressing
2 teaspoons lemon juice, fresh

2 tablespoons plus 2
   teaspoons wine vinegar
1 clove garlic, crushed
½ pound tomato wedges
½ pound bell peppers, sliced
1 small red onion, sliced
½ bunch radishes, sliced
Parmesian cheese

Cook spaghetti. Combine first nine ingredients and mix with spaghetti. Add tomatoes, bell pepers, onion and radishes. Best if made the day before and mixed again beofre serving and garnish with tomato slices and Parmesian cheese.

Betty Ferber   *Rowland High School, Rowland Heights*

Wilted Spinach Salad

Serves 4 to 6

1 pound spinach
½ pound mushrooms
4 slices bacon
¼ cup vinegar
½ teaspoon salt
2 cloves garlic, minced

¼ teaspoon coarsely ground pepper
¼ teaspoon oregano
⅛ teaspoon dry mustard
¼ teaspoon basil
½ teaspoon sugar

Wash spinach, tear leaves off stems and drain on paper towels. Turn spinach leaves into bowl. Wipe mushrooms with a damp cloth, slice lengthwise and add to spinach. Fry bacon until crisp. Remove from skillet and crumble coarsely. Combine vinegar, salt, garlic, pepper, oregano, mustard, basil and sugar. Heat bacon fat remaining in skillet. Add vinegar mixture, pouring carefully so dressing does not splatter. Pour hot dressing over spinach, toss well and sprinkle with crumbled bacon. Serve at once.

"This is my husband's favorite salad!"

Pam Ford   **Temecula Valley High School**
Temecula

Mrs. Traw's Best-Ever Baked Beans

Serves 8

21-oz. can pork and beans,
    drain off liquid
1 teaspoon salt
⅛ teaspoon pepper
2 tablespoons brown sugar

½ cup catsup
1 tablespoon vinegar
1 tablespoon Worcestershire sauce
½ medium size onion, diced

Combine all ingredients in a 2-quart casserole dish. Cover with glass lid or plasstic wrap. Microwave on reheat for 12 to 14 minutes or until mixture bubbles. Let stand, covered, 3 minutes before serving. May be baked in conventional oven at 350⁰ for 55 minutes.

"My Mom has made this recipe for years. It goes great with BBQ'd hamburgers, steaks or ribs."

Marianne Traw   **Ball Junior High School**
Anaheim

New England Style Baked Beans

Serves 6 to 8

12 slices thick-sliced bacon,
    cut into 1" lengths
¼ cup onion, chopped
½ cup celery, diced
3 14 to 16-oz. cans pork and beans
    with tomato sauce

1/3 cup chili sauce, catsup or
    bottled barbeque sauce
2 tablespoons brown sugar or
    molasses
2 tablespoons pickle relish, drained
cooked bacon curls, if desired

Saute bacon in frying pan over low heat until about 2/3 done. Drain bacon pieces on absorbent paper. drain off all but 2 tablespoons of the drippings. Add onion and celery to frying pan and cook slowly until tender. Add remaining ingredients except bacon curls and 1/3 of the bacon pieces; mix carefully.

Pour into a 1½ quart casserole dish. Sprinkle remaining bacon over top of beans; cover. Bake in preheated 350⁰ oven until beans are heated, 35 to 40 minutes. If preferred, beans may be heated in a frying pan on top of the stove for 25 to 30 minutes. Stir as needed. Serve, garnished with additional bacon curls, if desired.

Marcy Bergner   *Kearny High School, San Diego*

Crock of Beans

Serves 12

¾ pound ground beef	1 cup catsup
¾ 1-pound bacon, chopped	¼ cup brown sugar
1 small onion, chopped	3 tablespoons white vinegar
1 16-oz. can kidney beans	1 tablespoon liquid smoke
1 16-oz. can lima or butter beans	1 teaspoon salt
2 16-oz. cans baked beans	

Cook beef; drain and place in crock pot. Fry chopped bacon; drain most of the fat, but leave enough to saute chopped onion. Place in crock pot. Add remaining ingredients to pot and mix together. Cook on low setting 4 to 6 hours. Excellent with burgers, hot dogs, polish sausage or such.

"Make ahead and serve right from the pot! Stays nice and hot!"

Jeanne Koerner   *Rowland High School*
                                                       Rowland Heights

Onions First

Serves 4 to 6

3 large purple onions	½ teaspoon salt
1 lemon	2 to 3 large tomatoes, sliced
½ cup salad oil	1 cucumber, sliced
¼ cup wine vinegar	coarsely ground pepper
2 tablespoons lemon juice	snipped parsley
1 teaspoon savory	

Cut onions and lemon in paper thin slices. Arrange in layers in a small bowl. Combine oil, vinegr, lemon juice, savory and salt. Pour over onion and lemon slices. Chill 8 hours or overnight, stirring occasionally. Drain and reserve dressing.

At serving time, line platter with lettuce and arrange tomatoes and cucumbers around edge with onions in the center. Drizzle tomatoes and cucumbers with dressing and dash with pepper and sprinkle with parsley.

"Goes great with hamburgers cooked outside for a picnic!"

Alcyone Bass   *Hamilton Junior High School*
                                                     Long Beach

126

Cheese Scalloped Potatoes
(Using a food processor)

Serves 8

8 oz. cheddar cheese or
   American cheese
¼ cup margarine
¼ cup flour
2 cups milk

1 teaspoon salt
¼ teaspoon pepper
5 medium potatoes, peel
   if desired
2 small yellow onions

Preheat oven to 350⁰. Position disc in processor with shredding side up and shred cheese. Set aside.

In a 2-quart saucepan, melt butter over low heat. Bend in flour. Add milk all at once and cook stirring constantly until slightly thickened. Add shredded cheese.

Season and continue to cook, stirring, until cheese melts. Remove from heat. Spread half the cheese sauce on bottom of shallow 2½-quart baking dish.

Position disc in processor with slicing side up and slice potatoes and onions. As vegetables reach fill level, empty into baking dish. Arrange potato and onion slices over cheese sauce. Spread remaining cheese sauce over top. Bake until potatoes are tender, about 1 hour.

Marianne Traw
                                                           Ball Junior High School
                                                                  Anaheim

Relaxed Chicken

Serves 10 to 12

1½ cups soy sauce
½ cup water
¼ cup salad oil
¼ cup gin
1 finger fresh ginger root, peeled

2 cloves garlic, peeled
1/3 cup sugar
3 small fryers, quartered, or enough
   drumsticks, breasts and thighs to
   feed 10 to 12 people

Place soy sauce, water, oil, gin, peeled ginger root, peeled garlic and sugar in blender. Blend on high until garlic and ginger are in fine particles and marinade is somewhat thickened. (This can be put together without a blender, but the ginger must be shredded and the garlic minced. Also, the consistency will be thinner.)

Arrange chicken parts in a large plastic container which can be sealed (Tupperware), or in a sealable plastic bag. Pour marinade over chicken, coating each piece thoroughly. Marinate a minimum of 2 hours, but overnight or all day is better. Be sure to refrigerate and turn occasionally.

Place marinated chicken in wire basket and fasten to spit to revolve over large, but low fire (no hood). May be done flat on regular grill, but more turning is required and will be a little drier. Baste with remaining marinade until chicken is done, 1 to 1½ hours.

Any remaining marinade will keep in a jar in the refrigerator for a week or two to do a smaller "family" batch of chicken.

"The gin makes the chicken *relaxed* and so tender . . . and you'll be too, because it's so easy!"

Betsy Cosart
                                                                 Monache High School
                                                                        Porterville

Lemon Chicken

Serves 8 to 10

2 to 3 pound frying chickens,
   skinned, cut up for barbeque
1 cube butter or margarine, melted with
   ¼ cup lemon juice
2 teaspoons salt

2 teaspoons sugar
¼ teaspoon pepper
¼ teaspoon paprika
¼ teaspoon garlic powder

Soak chicken in oil at least ½ hour before cooking (drain well). Mix spices together. Grill chicken 15 to 20 minutes on *both* sides. Turn and baste with lemon butter sauce and sprinkle with spices. Cook 10 minutes, turn, baste, sprinkle. Cook 10 minutes, turn baste, sprinkle. Cook 10 minutes. Entire cooking time should be from 1 hour 10 minutes to 1 hour 20 minutes, depending on how well done you want it. This is done on a *Weber* or covered barbeque.

If there are any leftovers, it can be frozen and microwaved for reheating.

Angie Garrett   **Tenaya Middle School, Fresno**

Meat Marinade

Serves 4 to 6

¼ cup salad oil
¼ cup catsup
2 tablespoons terragon vinegar
½ teaspoon salt

dash pepper
1 clove garlic, sliced
1½ to 2 pounds thick cut sirloin
   steak

Combine first 6 ingredients. Pour over a thick cut of sirloin. Let set for 3 hours, turning every half hour. Barbeque for 20 minutes on each side.

"We use this delicious meat marinade for every barberque occasion.

JoAnn Gonzales   **Hesperia High School**
                                            Hesperia

Barbecue Cups

Serves 8

¾ pound ground beef
½ cup barbecue sauce
1 tablespoon instant minced onion

1 8-oz. can refrigerated
   biscuits
¾ cup cheddar cheese, shredded

In a large skillet, brown ground beef and drain. Add barbecue sauce and onion. Set aside.

Separate biscuit dough into 10 ungreased muffin cups pressing dough up both sides to the edge of the cup. Spoon meat mixture into cups. Sprinkle each with cheese. Bake at 400º for 10 to 12 minutes until golden brown.

"We made these in our 7th grade foods class. They are very simple to prepare and delicious.'

Marianne Traw   **Ball Junior High School**
                                           Anaheim

128

Barbecue Rib Sauce

Serves 4 to 5

6 pounds pork ribs
salt and pepper
¼ cup sugar
¼ cup dark brown sugar
2 cups water
¼ cup white vinegar
13 cup mustard

1/3 cup Worcestershire sauce
¼ cup soy sauce
2½ tablespoons liquid smoke
1 16-oz. can tomato sauce
2 cloves garlic, crushed
2 tablespoons Jalapeno chili
    peppers, diced

In a saucepan, mix together sugar, brown sugar, water, vinegar, mustard, Worcestershire sauce, soy sauce, liquid smoke, tomato sauce, garlic and Jalapeno peppers. Cook over medium heat, stirring constinually, until mixture comes to a boil. Then simmer for 1 hour, uncovered.

Season ribs with salt and pepper. Marinate with sauce for 4 to 5 hours (optional). Remove ribs and save sauce for basting. Cook ribs on grill or rotisserie on low heat for approximately 2 hours or until done. Baste while cooking.

Leota Hill   *Saddleback High School*
                                                           Santa Ana

Korean Shortrib Barbecue

Serves 4

4 pounds well-trimmed beef
    shortribs cut at 2½" intervals
½ cup soy sauce
½ cup water
¼ cup green onions, sliced
    (includes tops)

2 tablespoons sesame seed
2 tablespoons sugar
2 cloves garlic, minced
½ teaspoon pepper

With bone side down, dice-cut the 2½" shortrib cubes as follows: Cut meat halfway to the bone every ½" in one direction, at right angles, cut every ½" but only go ½" deep. To make the marinade: Combine the soy sauce, water, onions, sesame seed, sugar, garlic and pepper. Place scored pieces of meat into marinade and chill covered in the refrigerator 4 to 5 hours.

Place meat bone side down, on the barbecue grill over high heat. When brown, turn and cook on the meat side. Lift and turn meat throughout cooking time, about 5 minutes, to expose all surfaces to the heat. Cook until crisply browned and done to your preference. Have plenty of napkins on hand and eat while hot.

"I have used steaks with this marinade, too!"

Marcy Bergner   *Kearny High School*
                                                           San Diego

Texas Barbeque Sauce

Makes 2 pints

1 tablespoons chili powder
2 tablespoons flour
1 teaspoon garlic salt
¼ cup Worcestershire sauce
1/3 cup waffle syrup

½ cup catsup
1 teaspoon liquid smoke
2 cups water
2 tablespoons butter

In a saucepan, mix together chili powder, flour and salt. Add Worcestershire sauce, waffle syrup, catsup, liquid smoke, water and butter. Simmer on low heat for one hour.

"You can add shredded roast beef and let simmer for several hours to make a terrific barbeque sandwich. It's also great to use on the grill for chicken and beef!"

Linda Hinson   *Diegueno Junior High School*
                                                    Encinitas

Steuart Steak Flambe

Serves 6 to 8

⅛ cup rock salt   1 cup brandy
Tri-tip (beef cut)   BBQ
coarse ground pepper   Cast iron skillet
1 cube butter

Trim excess fat from Tri-tip, moisten with water and sprinkle cracked, coarse pepper all around the Tri-tip.

Start BBQ grill. Using a heavy cast iron skillet, sprinkle rock salt in bottom of skillet. (Just enough to cover lightly.) Place skillet on BBQ grill and heat for about 5 to 10 minutes. Salt will start to pop when hot.

Add Tri-tip on top of rock salt. Sear both sides of meat for 5 mniutes on *each side*. Remove meat from skillet and set aside on plate. Add 1 cube butter to skillet and melt. Return Tri-tip to skillet, with melted butter. Sear meat for *5 minutes on each side*.

Carefully add 1 cup brandy to skillet and flambe. After fire recedes, cover pan or use BBQ lid and continue searing meat for 5 minutes more on each side. Remove from heat and let Tri-tip rest for 3 to 5 minutes before slicing. Sauteed mushrooms and onions are a must with this dish.

Jean Steuart   *Sanger High School*
                                                    Sanger

Teriyaki Burgers

Serves 6

1 1-pound 4½-oz. can sliced pineapple   ¼ teaspoon garlic powder
¼ cup pineapple juice   ¼ teaspoon salt
1/3 cup soy sauce   2 tablespoons minced onion
1 teaspoon ginger   2 pounds ground beef
1 teaspoon sugar

Drain pineaple, saving ¼ cup juice. Combine soy sauce, ginger, sugar, garlic powder and salt. Stir together until sugar is dissolved. Add 3 tablespoons of this mixture and minced onion to the meat. Mix thoroughly. Form patties and cook close to hot coals on hibachi or barbecue. When patties are turned, dip a pineapple slice into the teriyaki sauce and place on hamburger while second side is cooking. Serve on buttered, toasted buns with mustard, catsup or relish.

"These burgers are great with cole slaw and baked beans!"

Pam Ford   *Temecula Valley High School*
                                                    Temecula
130

All-American Chocolate Cake

Serves 12 to 15

2 cups sugar, sifted
2 cups flour, sifted
1 stick margarine or ½ cup
½ cup shortening
4 tablespoons cocoa
1 cup water

2 eggs, slightly beaten
½ cup buttermilk or ½ cup milk
   plus 1½ teaspoons vinegar
1 teaspoon soda
1 teaspoon cinnamon (optional)
1 teaspoon vanilla

In a bowl place sugar and flour; set aside. In a sauce pan put margarine, shortening, cocoa and water. Bring to a boil, then add to flour and sugar. Mix well. Add beaten eggs, buttermilk, soda, cinnamon and vanilla and mix well, then pour into a 9" x 13" greased pan. Bake at 350⁰ for 25 minutes.

Frosting
Make while cake is baking and frost while still *hot.*

1 stick margarine or ½ cup
4 tablespoons cocoa
1/3 cup milk

3½ cups powdered sugar
1 teaspoon vanilla
nuts, if desired

Melt in a sauce pan, margarine, cocoa and milk. Remove from heat and add powdered sugar, vanilla and nuts. Beat well and spread on hot cake still in pan.

"This fast and easy cake is wonderful for any holiday dessert. Frosting sets up like fudge candy."

Marie Humphrey

Grant School
Escondido

Banana Split Cake

Serves 30 to 35

1 yellow cake mix
1 5⅝-oz. **instant** vanilla pudding
2 cups milk
2 8-oz. packages cream cheese,
   room temperature
6 to 8 bananas, chilled

2 20-oz. cans crushed pineapple,
   drained and chilled
2 8-oz. containers Cool Whip,
   thawed
2 10-oz. packages frozen strawberries,
   (fresh are better), thawed and drained

Prepare cake mix as directed and bake in a 12" x 18" pan, or two 9" x 13" pans, for only 15 to 17 minutes. Cool cake. Mix pudding with only 2 cups milk. Blend cream cheese into pudding. Spread this mixture onto cake. Cut up bananas in small pieces on top of pudding/cheese spread. Spread crushed pineapple over top of bananas. Spread Cool Whip over top of pineapple and place strawberries on top of Cool Whip.

"This may be used for Fourth of July by covering the upper left corner with well-drained blueberries topped with 'stars' of Cool Whip and placing the strawberries as 'stripes' across the cake which has been spread with Cool Whip to resemble a flag."

Jean Jeter

Park View Intermediate
Lancaster

131

Fourth of July Cheesecakes

Serves 12
(A microwave recipe!)

2 8-oz. packages cream cheese	2 tablespoons vanilla
2/3 cup sugar	12 vanilla wafers
2 eggs	1 can cherry pie filling (or
2 tablespoons lemon juice	blueberry or half and half)

Soften cream cheese in 1 quart microwave-safe bowl on medium for 1½ minutes. beat in sugar, eggs, lemon juice and vanilla until light and fluffy.

Line a micro-muffin pan for 6 (or 6 custard cups) with paper liners. Place a vanilla wafer in the bottom of each liner and fill ¾ full with cream cheese mixture. Cook on medium in microwave for two minutes, rotating dish once.

Top each with two tablespoons pie filling. Chill until set.

Martha Ford   *T. Roosevelt Junior High School*
Glendale

Chocolate-Covered Frozen Bananas

Serves 12

firm ripe bananas	chocolate topping
nuts, chopped	

Cut peeled bananas in half crosswise. Impale on wooden skewers and place in a freezer for one half hour or until thoroughly chilled. Remove bananas from freezer a few at a time. Dip and roll banana in melted chocolate topping, making sure that alll banana surfaces are completely covered. Shake or twirl banana before removing from pan to remove excess coating. While coating is still soft, roll the banana in chopped nuts. If coating becomes too hard to hold decorations, apply a little warm coating to back of nuts and hold in place until it sets. When covering sets, place bananas on squares of foil and wrap securely and store in freezer until ready to eat.

Chocolate Topping

1 12-oz. package semi-sweet chocolate pieces	6 tablespoons salad oil

Melt chocolate in top of double boiler over hot — not boiling — water. Add oil and stir until smooth. Keep warm over hot water while dipping.

Jane Van Wagoner   *Walnut High School, Walnut*

Cinnamon Stars

Makes 5 dozen

6 egg whites	1 pound ground almonds
1 pound powdered sugar	1 tablespoon cinnamon

Beat egg whites until stiff. Add powdered sugar, ground almonds and cinnamon. Thoroughly chill dough. Divide dough into thirds. Roll out on a board covered with an equal mixture of granulated sugar and flour. Cut out with star cookie cutter and place on a greased cookie sheet. Bake at 350° for 10 minutes.

"Simple to prepare as well as an extremely unique cookie and a delicious change from other cookie recipes!"

Bonnie Shrock   *Kearny High School, San Diego*

132

Fantastic Fruit Pizza

Serves 12

1 package yellow cake mix
2/3 cup graham cracker crumbs
½ cup nuts, chopped
½ cup butter, softened
1 egg

Filling
1 6-oz. package cream cheese
2/3 cup sugar
2 cups whipping cream
½ cup apple jelly, melted
assorted fresh fruit (sliced
    bananas, peaches, strawberries,
    melon balls)

Heat oven to 350⁰. In a large bowl, combine cake mix, cracker crumbs, nuts and butter at low speed until crumbly. Blend in egg. Press mixture in ungreased 12″ or 14″ pizza pan. Bake at 350⁰ for 12 to 15 minutes or until golden brown. Cool. While cooling make filling.

Filling
In a small bowl, beat cream cheese until fluffy. Gradually add sugar. Blend well. Beat in whipping cream until soft peaks form. Spread cream mixture on cooled crust. Arrange fruit as desired on top. Brush with melted jelly. Cut into wedges. Refrigerate leftovers.

Jane Schaffer and Barbara Skiles   *Santana High School, Santee*

Homemade Ice Cream

Makes about 1 gallon

4 eggs
4 pints half and half or
    light cream

1 cup to 1-1/3 cups sugar, granulated
2 tablespoons vanilla

Blend all ingredients in a blender using only 1 pint of half and half. Pour mixture into a gallon ice cream freezer and add the rest of the half and half. Mix well. Freeze according to freezer directions.

Variations: *For chocolate, add 1 cup Nestles Quick to above ingredients.*

"A Fourth of July tradition in my small, mid-western hometown!"

Carolyn Crum   *Newhart Junior High School*
Mission Viejo

Mint Ice Cream Frozen Dessert

Serves 12 to 15

1 package chocolate mint
    sandwich cookies
1 cup butter
3 cups powdered sugar

4 eggs, well beaten
3 squares unsweetened
    baking chocolate, melted
½ gallon vanilla ice cream

Freeze chocolate mint cookies, then crush in a food processor. Spread on the bottom of a 9″ x 12″ pan, reserving ½ cup for topping. cream butter, powdered sugar and eggs. Add melted chocolate, mix well and spread over cookie layer. Soften ice cream and spoon over chocolate layer. Garnish with remaining cookie crumbs. Freeze overnight.

"Cool and refreshing for a hot summr day!"

Gloria Reece   *Porterville High School, Porterville* 133

Fresh Peach Torte

Serves 6

3 egg whites
1 teaspoon vanilla
1 cup sugar
dash salt
1 teaspoon baking powder

½ saltine crackers, crushed
1 cup nuts, chopped
1½ cups fresh sliced peaches or 1
   large can peaches, chilled
whipped cream or Cool Whip

Beat eggs until foamy. Add vanilla and salt and continue to beat until stiff peaks form. Fold in baking powder, crumbs, and nuts. Put in a well-greased pie dish. Push higher at sides. Bake at 300° for 40 minutes. Cool completely. Drain peaches and place in pie shell and cover with Cool Whip. Chill.

"This is a delicious treat with fresh peaches. Also works well during the winter season."

Betty Ann Lawson

Valencia High School
Placentia

Pineapple Delight

Serves 8 to 12

1 #303 can crushhed pineapple
1 1-pound box vanilla wafers
2 eggs
½ cup butter, softened

1½ cups powdered sugar
sliced walnuts
1 large non-dairy topping or
   ½ pint whipping cream

Drain the canned pineapple. Grease an 8" x 8" pan. Crush wafers, and spread ¾ of them in the pan. Beat eggs, and gradually add butter and powdered sugar. Mix until thick. Spread egg mixture on top of crushed wafers. Place drained pineapple on top of egg mixture, then top with sliced walnuts. Spread whipped cream on top of walnuts and then remaining wafers on top of cream. Chill at least 2 hours before serving.

Jennifer Gierman

Ball Junior High School
Anaheim

Special Strawberry Dessert

Serves 12

1 Jiffy yellow cake mix
1 8-oz. cream cheese, room temperature
2 cups milk

1 small package instant vanilla
   pudding
1 pint strawberries, sliced
1 large non-dairy topping

Make cake according to directions on package using a 9" x 13" pan. Cool. Cream cream cheese and milk together until smooth. Add pudding and stir until thick. Spread over cake, add strawberries and non-dairy topping.

"A cool and refreshing dessert."

Brenda Umbro

San Marcos Junior High School
San Marcos

Strawberry Whipped Cream Cake

Serves a group

1 box white cake mix
1 10-oz. box frozen sliced
   strawberries, partially thawed
1 3-oz. package strawberry gelatin

3 cups whipping cream, whipped or
   1 large Cool Whip
2 bananas

Follow package directions to prepare batter. Pour into 2 9"-square pans or 9" x 13" pan with about 1¼ cups batter. Cool for 1 hour. While cooling cake, mix gelatin with 1 cup boiling water. Add 1 cup ice and stir to dissolve. Add partially thawed berries and stir to finish thawing. Refrigerate or put into freezer stirring every 10 to 15 minutes until almost set. Spread gelatin over cooled cake. Slice bananas thinly and layer over gelatin. Spread whipped cream over top of bananas, completely covering bananas. Cover with plastic wrap and keep refrigerated.

"It's really better 2 to 3 days after it's made, if you can keep people out of it that long!"

Polly Frank

**Lakewood High School
Lakewood**

Easy Strawberry Pie

Serves 6

1 graham cracker crust shell
32 marshmallows
½ cup milk

1 package frozen strawberries,
   sliced
½ cup walnuts
1 cup whipped cream (dessert whip)

Line a pie tin with graham cracker crust. Melt marshmallows in the milk in a double boiler. Let cook, add nuts and then strawberries. Let cool. Fold in whipped cream. Fill crumb shell. Sprinkle top with crumbs, if desired.

Lou Helen Yergat

**Mission Viejo High School
Mission Viejo**

Strawberry Smackers

Serves 9

1 teaspoon unflavored gelatin
½ cup cold water

2 cups strawberry yogurt
18 graham cracker squares

In a small pan, soften gelatin in water. Cook until completely dissolved. Combine yogurt with gelatin mixture. Line a 9" x 9" square pan with foil. Place half the crackers on foil and pour yogurt mixture over them. Carefully place remaining crackers on yogurt. Cover and freeze. Cut to desired-size sandwiches.

"A refreshing treat, especially when using your favorite flavor of yogurt!"

Susan Waterbury

**San Luis Obispo High School
San Luis Obispo**

Laura's Texas Cake

Serves a group

1¾ cups flour
½ teaspoon salt
1 teaspoon baking soda
2 eggs
½ cup sour cream

2 cups sugar
2 sticks margarine
1 cup water
4 tablespoons cocoa

Measure and sift together flour, salt and baking soda. Cream together eggs, sour cream and sugar. Beat in flour mixture. Set aside. In a saucepan, bring to a boil the margarine, water and cocoa. Add at once to the flour mixture and mix well. Pour into a greased 10" x 15" sheet cake pan. Bake at 350⁰ for 20 to 25 minutes or until done.

Icing

1 box powdered sugar
1 tablespoon vanilla
1 cup nuts, chopped

1 stick margarine
6 tablespoons milk
4 tablespoons cocoa

In a bowl, combine powdered sugar, vanilla and chopped nuts; set aside. In a saucepan, bring to a boil the margarine, milk and cocoa. Add at once to the powdered sugar mixture; stir well. Ice cake right out of the oven.

Janet Griffith   *Norco High School, Norco*

Fresh Cauliflower Salad (Labor Day)

Serves 10

4 cups cauliflower flowerettes,
    sliced
½ cup onion, chopped
½ cup bell pepper, chopped
2/3 cup dairy sour cream
3 tablespoons mayonnaise

1 teaspoon dry mustard
1 teaspoon sugar
1 tablespoon fresh dill, snipped *or*
    few dashes hot pepper sauce
2 medium tomatoes, seeded and
    chopped
few dashes hot pepper sauce

In a large bowl stir together the cauliflower, onion and green pepper. Combine the sour cream, mayonnaise, mustard, sugar, dill, and hot pepper sauce. Season to taste with salt and pepper. Gently stir dressing into vegetable mixture. Cover and chill several hours. Just before serving, carefully stir tomatoes into salad.

"This makes a great summer side dish when you are barbecuing steak or chicken."

Clyle Alt   *Bell Gardens High School*
Bell Gardens

Onions in Madeira Cream (Labor Day)

serves 6 to 8

4 large mild onions, thickly
   sliced
8 tablespoons butter
½ cup Madeira wine

salt and pepper to tste
¼ cup heavy cream
¼ cup fresh parsley, finely
   chopped

Melt butter in wide, heavy pan.Add the onion slices and turn them in the butter to coat them thoroughly. Cover the pan and cook over very low heat for 10 minutes, shaking pan occasionally. Uncover pan, increase the heat slightly and stir in the Madeira. Cook, stirring frequently until the Madeira evaporates and the onions are soft and lightly caramelized. Season to taste with salt and pepper and stir in the cream and parsley. Bring to a boil, then reduce heat and simmer 1 minute. Serve hot.

"The onions are marvelous with steak or any grilled meat."

Ginny Rocheleau
                                            Muirlands Junior High School
La Jolla

Smoked Beans (Labor Day)

Serves 12 to 15

1 pound ground beef
½ pound bacon, diced
2 32-oz. cans pork and beans
1 16-oz. can kidney beans,
   drained
1 cup catsup
¼ to ½ cup bar-b-que sauce
¼ cup brown sugar

1 tablespoon white vinegar
½ cup onions, diced
½ to 1 teaspoon salt
dash pepper
⅛ teaspoon chili pepper
1 teaspoon liquid smoke
1 clove garlic, minced

Brown hamburger and bacon; drain. Add all other ingredients into a slow cooker. Stir well to mix. Cook 5 to 6 hours on low. Serve hot.

Virginia A. Green
                                            Vista High School
Vista

Fruited Tuna Salad (Labor Day)

Serves 4

1 7-oz. can tuna, drained
1 cup pineapple tidbits, drained
1 cup seedless grapes
½ cup celery, diced
1 large can Chinese noodles

¼ cup pecans, chopped
3 tablespoons olives, thinly
   sliced
mayonnaise to moisten
lemon wedges

Break tuna in chunks. Combine with all remaining ingredients, but reserve enough noodles to sprinkle on the top of each salad. Use enough mayonnaise to lightly moisten. Serve on lettuce. Garnish with lemon wedges and whole pecans.

Ginny Rocheleau
                                            Muirlands Junior High School
La Jolla

Spaghetti Salad
(Columbus Day, October 14)

Serves 8 to 10

1 pound spaghetti, broken
½ red onion
½ bell pepper
1 cucumber, peeled

2 fresh tomatos
1 large bottle Italian dressing
1 8-oz. can tomato sauce
1 teaspoon salad seasoning

Cook spaghetti "aldente." Do not over cook. Chop all vegetables. Combine drained spaghetti and chopped vegetables in a large bowl. Pour dressing and tomato sauce into bowl. Add seasoning. Mix well; chill overnight.

"In honor of Christopher Columbus, we usually serve this American version of a spaghetti salad. Great for barbeques, too!"

JoAnn Gonzales   **Hesperia High School**
                                                      Hesperia

Teddy Bear Bow Tie Cookies
(Teddy Roosevelt's Birthday, October 27)

Serves 30 people (and hundreds of bears)

3 cups flour
2 tablespoons powdered sugar
3 eggs

1 tablespoon almond flavoring
oil for frying
powdered sugar for sprinkling

Combine flour, powdered sugar, eggs and almond flavoring. Knead for at least 10 minutes. This will be a *very* stiff dough, similar to noodle dough. Cover with plastic wrap and let stand at room temperature for at least 1 hour. Divide dough into 4 portions and roll each out paper thin. (If you have a pasta machine, this is the best way to get dough thin enough.) Cut into strips about 1" x 6". Twist each strip into a bow shape and pinch to secure. Fry the bows in 350° oil until lightly browned. Drain on paper towels. Sprinkle with powdered sugar, using a flour sifter to make an even coating.

"My teddy bears, 'Teddy Grable' and 'Vincent Van Bear,' just love these! All of your arctophiles will enjoy them, too!"

Gwenn Jensen   **Mira Mesa High School**
                                                    San Diego

Coconut Torte

Serves 6 to 9

½ cup butter or margarine
1 cup sugar
1½ cups vanilla wafer crumbs
   (1 12-oz. package = 3 cups crumbs)

3 eggs
1 cup pecans, chopped
1 3½-oz. can or 1½ cups
   flaked coconut

Cream butter and sugar until fluffy. Blend in vanilla wafer crumbs. Beat in eggs, one at a time. Stir in pecans and coconut. Turn into a greased and floured 9" round cake pan or an 2" x 8" x 8" square baking pan. Bake at 325° for 40 to 50 minutes. Cool and cut into wedges or squares. May be served with ice cream or whipped cream.

Nancy Welsh Parsons   **Millikan High School**
                                                       Long Beach

Carrot Cake (Election Day)

Serves 15 to 18

2 cups sugar
¾ cup oil
3 eggs
1 teaspoon vanilla
¾ cup buttermilk
2 cups carrots, grated
1 3½-oz. package coconut

1 15½-oz. can crushed pineapple,
   drained
2 cups flour
2 teaspoons baking soda
2 teaspoons cinnamon
1½ teaspoon salt
1 cup nuts, chopped

Mix sugar, oil, eggs, vanilla and buttermilk. Add carrots, coconut and pineapple. Combine flour, baking soda, cinnamon, salt and vanilla, mix well. Add chopped nuts. Pour into a 9" x 13" x 2" greased pan. Bake at 350° for 55 minutes or until done.

Icing

½ cup margarine
8 oz. cream cheese

1 teaspoon vanilla
1 pound powdered sugar

Combine all and mix in a bowl with a mixer until creamy. Cover cake while still in the pan.

Mrs. Kitty Worley

Norte Vista High School
Riverside

English Matrimonials (Boxing Day, December 26)

Makes 2 dozen small bars

½ cup butter
1 cup brown sugar
1½ cups flour
1 teaspoon baking soda

½ teaspoon salt
1¾ cups oatmeal
1½ cups jam or jelly

Mix all ingredients, except the jam or jelly, together. Put half of the mixture into a 9" x 13" baking pan. Warm the jam or jelly slightly, so that it will spread evenly and then spread it over the oatmeal mixture in the pan. Sprinkle remaining oatmeal mixture on the top and bake at 325° for 30 minutes or until bubbly around the edges. Cut into bars and cool thoroughly before serving.

"These are great with a pot of freshly brewed tea!"

Gwenn Jensen

Mira Mesa High School
San Diego

INDEX

143

ALPHABETIZED CONTRIBUTORS LIST

Allan, Joan, 69, 106
Los Cerritos Intermediate
Thousand Oaks

Alt, Clyle, 39, 64, 136
Bell Gardens High School
Bell Gardens

Armstrong, Lois, 109
Sonora High School
La Habra

Atkin, Anna, 55, 63
Monache High School
Porterville

Atkins, Marianne, 88
Faye Ross Junior High School
Cerritos

Baczynski, Kathie, 119
Mt. Carmel High School
San Diego

Bass, Alcyone, 81, 126
Hamilton Junior High School
Long Beach

Bechok, Priscilla, 50
Bell Gardens High School
Bell Gardens

Bergeron, Cathy, 89
Stanford Junior High School
Long Beach

Bergner, Marcy, 126, 129
Kearny High School
San Diego

Brown, Susan, 50
Sowers Middle School
Huntington Beach

Bruce, Libby, 25
Troy High School
Fullerton

Burke, Brenda, 28, 58
Mount Whitney High School
Visalia

Burkhart, Nanci, 3
Hueneme High School
Oxnard

Burns, Jeannie, 45
Los Osos Junior High School
Los Osos

Byrum, Nancy, 49
Patrick Henry High School
San Diego

Cain, Joy Nell, 52
Willowood Junior High School
West Covina

Campbell, Theresa, 41
Kennedy High School
La Palma

Chivers, Julie, 77
Tulare Union High School
Tulare

Cosart, Betsy, 74, 122, 127
Monache High School
Porterville

Crider, Erma Jean, 59, 118
Sanger High School
Sanger

Cronkhite, Mary, 6
Antelope Valley High School
Lancaster

Crum, Carolyn, 18, 133
Newhart Junior High School
Mission Viejo

Curfman. Astrid, 43
Newcomb Junior High School
Long Beach

Darnall, Marguerite S., 12, 102
Corona Senior High School
Corona

Daudistel, Kathleen, 88, 92
Hanford High School
Hanford

De Belius, Kathleen, 75
Mountain View High School
El Monte

Delap, Carole, 58, 100, 115
Golden West High School
Visalia

De Neve, Antoinette, 42
Jones Junior High School
Baldwin Park

Dever, Susan, 18
Bishop Union High school
Bishop

Estes, Marianne, 63, 101
La Mirada High School
La Mirada

Everitt, Diane, 114
Killingsworth Intermediate
Hawaiian Gardens

146

Umbro, Brenda, 15, 103, 134
San Marcos Junior High School
San Marcos

Van Camp, Nikki, 58
Poly High School
Riverside

Van Wagoner, Jane,, 23, 132
Walnut High School
Walnut

Vickers, Marion, 77
Bartlett Junior High School
Porterville

Walls, Millie, 4
El Dorado High School
Placentia

Waterbury, Susan, 34, 135
San Luis Obispo High School
San Luis Obispo

Wilcox, Shirley, 17, 30, 36
Burbank High School
Burbank

Willems, Connie, 35
Paulding Intermediate
Arroyo Grande

Williams, Helen W., 77
North High School
Bakersfield

Wilson, Debbie, 28, 38
Hueneme High School
Oxnard

Wilson, Dorothy, 110, 113
Dale Junior High School
Anaheim

Wilson, Vera, 13, 57
Del Dios Middle School
Escondido

Wisely, Marilyn, 38
Sparks Junior High School
La Puente

Wolfe, Patricia, 35, 51
Lakewood High School, Retired
Lakewood

Wood, J.J., 109
Stevens Junior High School
Long Beach

Worley, Kitty, 12, 139
Norte Vista High School
Riverside

Yackey, George, 89
Santana High School
Santee

Yergat, Lou Helen, 5, 19, 20, 117, 135
Mission Viejo High School
Mission Viejo